THE FUTURE OF WESTERN CIVILIZATION

PSYCHIATRIST DR NICHOLAS BEECROFT INTERVIEWS VISIONARY LEADERS

Series 1

Volumes 28, 29, 31, 33, 34, 35, 36

BOOK FOUR

The Future of Western Civilization:
Psychiatrist Dr Nicholas Beecroft Interviews Visionary Leaders
Series 1, Book 4. Volumes 28, 29, 31, 33, 34, 35, 36

ISBN-13: 978-1494732912
ISBN-10: 1494732912

Book design by Maureen Cutajar
www.gopublished.com

Contents

Future of Western Civilization Series Mission

I'm Dr Nicholas Beecroft, a Consultant Psychiatrist in London. I'm exploring the Future of Western Civilization through a series of interviews. I want us to rejuvenate our energy, direction and self-confidence as a Civilization. My mission is to create a positive, appreciative space in which leaders at the evolutionary edge of our Civilization can share their experience and set out their vision for our future to inspire others. They are visionaries sowing the seeds of future transformation, all genuine, creative, courageous people who care about whom we are and where we're going.

By "Civilization," I mean Western Civilization-the one I've lived in; to one that is transformed the world over the last 500 years; the one that has gone global; the one that faces enormous threats, challenges and has the unprecedented opportunity to evolve to an amazing future. When there's so much changing all at once, old structures failing and a huge array of emerging threats, that all generates a lot of anxiety, pessimism and fear which distract us from putting energy into creating new solutions, generating new ideas and envisioning a better future.

Behind the News Headlines, usually quietly, under the radar, there's a lot of good stuff going on; the seeds of the future taking root in the present. There are lots of evolutionaries trying out new ideas, new technologies, new ways of organizing and more integrated, conscious and balanced ways of thinking and being.

Western Civilization has been supremely successful in all kinds of ways of which we should be enormously proud. Science, technology, industrialization, democracy, individual rights, personal freedom, property rights, the rule of law, Christianity, humanism, organization, capitalism, feminism, civil rights, philosophy, music, art, even Imperialism have all, on balance, transformed the world for the better and have created new life conditions with new challenges and problems. In some cases, these advances

I

had nasty side effects and some have become imbalanced. In others, they have replaced older structures and beliefs, and many babies have been lost with the bathwater.

Human Civilization is made up of human beings who are conscious beings and physical animals, all interconnected like a shoal of fish or a flock of birds. I've interviewed a huge variety of people across a variety roles, professions, beliefs, politics, status, nationalities, religions, social classes and backgrounds. What is crystal clear to me is that whilst the world we live in is hyper-complex, we operate in it using a kind of mini-map of our Civilization in our minds which we use to navigate through the world, guided by our inner compass of intuition and rational thought. It is astonishing how similar these inner maps are, and the patterns are clear. This is how we self-organize in what is a complex living system-just like a beehive or wildebeest migration.

Now we are super-connected by the internet, media and travel. We carry in our pockets access to billions of people and to just about all the knowledge that ever existed. Turning inwards we have access to instinctive intuition, heart, wisdom, common sense and judgement. Put together, that represents vast human potential and the most amazing opportunity for personal and cultural evolution ever. Looked at like that, just about all of our shared challenges and threats are solvable and a much better world is highly realistic. We're engaged in conscious evolution of ourselves and our Civilization.

There is a huge range of threats and challenges to The West and to the whole World. People focus their attention on different ones depending on their situation, beliefs and emotional make-up. The list is pretty depressing and overwhelming-so I've turned it into a list of positive questions instead. Here's a start:

- Who are we?
- Where are we going?
- What kind of future do we envisage?
- How do we rise to the challenges we face?
- What do we believe; what is right, what is wrong, what is true, what is false? What do we value and desire?
- What do we love about our Civilization?

- What works well?
- What's worth preserving and defending?
- How can we be confidently patriotic, open, diverse and global at the same time?
- How do we restore a healthy authority in ourselves, our roles and institutions?
- How can we have authority which is fair, accountable, evidence-based and respectful of complexity?
- How can be apply science effectively to complex systems like the mind, consciousness, society without oversimplification?
- How do we get sustainable, secure, clean energy?
- How do we make the welfare state to be fair to taxpayers and empowering to recipients?
- How do we balance individual rights with group responsibilities?
- Shall we start having enough children to sustain our future without depending on immigration?
- How do we absorb huge flows of immigration into a confident, open, dynamic, cohesive and secure country?
- How can we be comfortable and secure with our complex, overlapping identities?
- How do we innovate, reorganize, get our way out of recession?
- How do we enjoy the growth of human potential in harmony with the planet upon which we depend ?
- How do we evolve capitalism to serve our culture and values more holistically and fairly?
- How do we rehumanize medicine to get the best of technology whilst having compassion and healing and open our minds to the huge non-linear, non-reductionist possibilities?
- How do we refresh our democracy to deepen it rather than have occasional elections manipulated by narrow interest groups, political cabals and the media?
- Who are successful examples of organic leadership-leadership in line with human nature including self-organizing living systems, trust, respect, judgement, intuition?
- What can we learn from pioneers in consciousness and cultural evolution?
- How can we most effectively support our cultural evolution, healthy attitude to risk, judgment and responsibility?

- How do we support the evolution for a more mature, more conscious post-partisan politics which integrates left and right, individual and group, power and love, freedom and security, justice and fairness?
- How can we integrate the dark, shadow side of our history so as to unlock our power and potential?
- How do we intelligently integrate what we have come to think of as science with intuition, wisdom and complexity?
- How do we preserve and improve our open, free, democratic, pluralistic society whilst living with other cultures which actively assert their righteousness, supremacy and desire for dominance over us?
- How do we rebalance our economies to live within our means, to support the development of the emerging economies whilst remaining competitive and vibrant?
- How do we live ecologically sustainably?
- How do we have a post-postmodern spirituality which honors life and spirit and which transcends and includes existing religions and secular views?
- How do we evolve from a culture of entitlement to a culture of empowerment, maximizing potential, freedom with fairness and responsibility?
- How do we emerge beyond patriarchy and feminism to a mature, conscious masculinity and femininity, embodied, equal but different, comfortable with our inter-penetrating Yin and Yang?
- How do we re-legitimize judgement; not prejudice but healthy judgement of right and wrong, good and bad as the foundation of autonomy, freedom and authority?
- How do we get healthy hierarchies which are empowering and adaptive?
- How do we create new fields of consciousness; our energetic potential into which the future will emerge-create the field of alignment and remove the obstacles and provide the support structures and allow the self-organization to occur?
- What's already here and happening…
- What new technologies are coming which will change our way of life and opportunities?
- What are the values and beliefs of emerging new generations around the world?

- How do we foresee or create the future?
- How can we boost our cultural direction and confidence?
- Where we are fighting, what are we fighting for?
- How can we make our Civilization so attractive that others choose to align with us, emulate us and synergize with us?
- What disruptive technologies are going to change our world?
- How can we live in harmony with the planet whilst continuing to evolve our way of life?
- How can we securely and confidently live with Islam at home and abroad while it goes through its turbulent period of evolution?
- How do we ensure that the basics of food, water, clean air, energy, health and education are available fairly to everyone?
- How do we evolve wrongs of racism, nationalism, imperialism without simply inverting them to become the future victims new racisms, nationalisms and fascisms from other cultures?
- How do we deal with growing geopolitical assertiveness and military build-up by China, India, Pakistan, Russia, Iran, Brazil, Turkey, South Africa?
- Can we make use of raw materials sustainably?
- How do we stay safe with continuing nuclear proliferation to Iran, North Korea and others?
- How do we clear our massive sovereign and personal debts and live within our means?
- How can we evolve the way we do welfare, health and social care to make them affordable and more supportive of a healthy society?
- How do we enjoy the benefits of capitalism without being debt-slaves and making sure we value family, community, health, environment, education, security, freedom and human potential?
- How can we rejuvenate the family as the cornerstone of our culture?
- How do great teachers inspire, empower and carry authority in classrooms?
- How can we compete with the very determined educational competition from the East?
- How do we bring in the alienated into the mainstream with dignity and compassion?
- How do we make taxation and welfare fair for hardworking taxpayers?

5

- How can we eat more healthy, natural food, connected to its production whilst making it fun and practical?
- How can we farm animals in a kind, healthy way?
- How can we make care homes wonderful, heavenly places full of life, stimulation and family?
- How can hospitals empower, support and care for their staff so that they, in turn, are fit to care for their patients?
- How can we value wellbeing over objects?
- Can we revalue fatherhood and motherhood?
- Can we value life and the human spirit in a way which is inclusive of all religions, spiritualities, humanism and atheism?
- How can our organizations maximize their human potential and help their team to live their purpose and values?
- Can we restore an innocent, playful, magical childhood?
- Can we reweave community by choice or is it something we only do when we have no choice?
- Who does empowering, inspiring, visionary, values-driven, spirit-kindling leadership?
- How do we balance our budgets and trade?
- ......And so on!

Acknowledgements

The Future of Western Civilization Series of interviews is the product of much work, many conversations and experiences over the preceding 30 years. Huge thanks to Melanie Mortiboys who has been fundamental to the project, it's conception, its incubation, birth and delivery. She has been there at every step of the way with encouragement, support, wisdom and good judgement.

The public face of the project, embodied in the series of interviews with visionary leaders got going in early 2011 with the first interview with William Nkata Masembe on the subject of patriotism from a newcomer's perspective. Many thanks to Nkata for being the first to boldly put himself on the line before the project was established.

Thank you to all those who took part in the subsequent Future of Western Civilization interviews: Melanie Mortiboys, Joseph McCormick, Martin Rutte, Dr Mary Gentile, Professor Jim Garrison, Dr Elisabet Sahtouris, Traci Fenton, Howard Bloom, Andrew Cohen, Dr Robin Wood, Chris Parish, Dr Don Beck, Herb Meyer, Neil Howe, Lynne McTaggart, Peggy Holman, Richard Barrett, Bishop Michael Nazir-Ali, Adrian Wagner, Joshua Gorman, Dr Robin Youngson, Jordan MacLeod, Mark Walsh, Soleira Green, Jim Rough, Joshua Gorman, Peter Merry, Helen Titchen Beeth, Barnaby Flynn, Danny Lambert, John Bunzl, Jon Freeman, Phil Neisser, Jacob Hess, Georgeanne Lamont, Peter Smith, Angeline Ruredzo, Steve Boley and Masana De Souza.

Behind the scenes, many people have been involved in the Future of Western Civilization project. Thanks to Linda Beecroft, Mike Beecroft, Cherie Beck, Dr Don Beck, Andrew Booth, Andrew Campbell, Chris Collins, Howard Donenfeld, Soleira Green, Samuel Humphreys, Jane MacAllister, Matthew McGuinness, Jan Mattsson, Hannah Mortiboys, Chris Parish, Martin Rutte, Lyndsey Wall, Matthew Wall, Dick Werling and Dr Robin Wood for their support and encouragement. Covers by Tatiana Villa. Formatting by Maureen Cutajar.

Dr Nicholas Beecroft

I'm a Consultant Psychiatrist. I trained as a doctor at Guy's and St Thomas's Medical School in London, doing a BSc. in psychology at University College as part of my medical degree. After a year as a House Physician and House Surgeon, I went straight into psychiatry at the Maudsley Hospital, the Institute of Psychiatry in London where I became a member of the Royal College of Psychiatrists.

I specialize in organizational and military psychiatry and have worked with the British Army, the Royal Navy and the National Health Service.

I spent 5 years developing an interest in what I came to call "Organic Leadership," aligning organizations with human nature to unleash maximum human potential. I developed this through a combination of consulting, coaching and teaching across a wide range of organizations including McKinsey & Co., BP, Cable & Wireless, the National Health Service, British Gas and Johannesburg City Council. I helped to establish the first Department of Organizational Psychiatry outside of the USA at King's College London where I taught executives and MSc. students Organizational Psychiatry and Psychology.

I have had a lifelong interest in Foreign Policy, national identity, security and geopolitics. Whilst I was at studying at the London Business School for an MBA, I watched the September 11, 2001 terrorist attacks live on television. This and the aftermath persuaded me that it was time to transform our Foreign Policy to include the human dimension-to perceive International relations as the interrelationships between individuals, groups and mass consciousness. I set about applying the knowledge and skills from clinical psychology, psychiatry and group dynamics to diplomacy and began to consult to diplomats, politicians and journalists. I called this "Psyplomacy."

I immersed myself in Track Two (off the record) diplomacy, helping to facilitate dialogue on immigration into Europe, the Weaponization of

Space, Western-Chinese relations, European Common Foreign and Security Policy, State-building, British-German relations, Public Diplomacy, peace building, Islamic radicalization and counter-terrorism.

I worked with the Foreign & Commonwealth Office in the British Embassy in Damascus where I put the British-Syrian relationship on the psychiatrist's couch, analyzing the relationship and recommending strategies to improve it.

I influenced the British Council in London to shift their model of public diplomacy from a marketing model to a relationships-based model grounded in a clear identity, values and authentic dialogue. They launched a new policy based upon the Psyplomacy model.

After the German Foreign Minister expressed his frustration at the treatment of Germany in the British media, he accepted my proposal to work with the German Embassy in London on a psychologically informed approach to public diplomacy to improve the British German relationship.

I helped to stimulate the debate within the British government and media about Britishness, patriotism and multiculturalism which is gradually been opening up over the last 10 years. I made a substantial commitment to work behind the scenes on our strategy for the "War on Terror" which I shared in a number of places including briefing two Foreign Secretaries, the Minister for International Development, the Conservative party, the BBC, Channel 4, the Ministry of Defense and the House of Commons Foreign Affairs Select Committee.

It became clear to me that, "We" the British and, more broadly, "We" Western Civilization had lost our direction and self-confidence. I began with a series of interviews with people which I called "Britain on the Couch." The key theme across the board was a perception of loss of confidence and authority. I interviewed teachers, doctors, nurses, military personnel and the general public to find out what is the foundation of their authority? What most fascinated me was that, in spite of coming from a very broad range of backgrounds, the people spoke as one as if singing from the same hymn sheet, I could almost sense and inner compass and map which everyone shared and-there was a big wobble in it! The traditional order and self-confidence arising from clear beliefs and shared identity had been breaking down but hadn't yet been replaced by a new set of beliefs and values. Culturally we have many old baggage and maladaptive beliefs which are limiting our full potential. If we going to succeed at a time of unprecedented global change then we can and need to step up to the next level of cultural and personal evolution.

I concluded that if we are to survive and thrive in the face of the many challenges which we face then we are going to have to sort ourselves out-to be clear about who we are, where we're going, what we believe, what is right, what is wrong, what is true, what is false; to restore our self-confidence, vision and values around which we can align.

I realized that to rejuvenate our society we would need a strong spiritual foundation. That was an uncomfortable conclusion for me because I considered myself to be undeveloped in that area. I was brought up to consider Christianity and spirituality to be a naive, unscientific, superstitious and rather embarrassing relic of the past which simply wasn't necessary in the modern world. However, through my explorations I realized that we need some core foundational truths about who we are as human beings, why we're here and how we should live. So, I set about a long journey of exploration through training in Energetics, Values analysis & facilitation, Transformative-Evolutionary Coaching, Vipassana meditation, Enlightenment Intensives, Tantra, Healing, Open Space Technology and Spiral Dynamics Integral. I participated in a Circle of Trust Courage to Lead retreat, the New Warrior Training Adventure, the Mankind Project, the Culture of Honoring Initiatory Journey and have attended many workshops on improvisation and comedy. The big questions are still largely a mystery to me but I'm a bit further forward in the enquiry.

There were three main conclusions that came out of all this. One was that for all the endless negativity in the media and public conversation about the huge range of problems and threats which exist, there are a huge number of people globally working on inspirational and initiatives, ideas and visions in what is a giant process of cultural evolution throughout emerging global consciousness. As Don Beck puts it, "No more prizes for predicting the rain. Its time to build the Ark."

The second main lesson was that it is a massive waste of time and energy when we resist that which we don't like. In a fierce battle with a Marxist professor which ended in stalemate, my opponent simply collapsed and dropped away when I asked him, "if everyone took up your ideas and if the world were the way you would like it to be, what would that be like?" He simply didn't know. He'd never considered it. He only knew what he was against, what he hated. He was like a windsock with no wind. I if that to defeat all those cultural forces which I had so fiercely resisted, I simply needed to leapfrog to the other side with that incisive question. The only problem was that I couldn't answer the question myself!

The third main lesson was that we as individuals and a group have much of our power and potential locked away in our shadow, in our dark side, the wounds, the taboos, the dysfunctional beliefs, false dichotomies and the groupthink. To unlock our potential, we need to heal those wounds and shine a light on the dark side and integrate the healthy strands of all. The old false dichotomies such as left and right, male and female, love and power, freedom and control, security and openness, diversity and unity, cohesion and separation, judgement and non-judgement, truth and mystery, patriotism and globalism each have healthy and unhealthy strands which need sorting out and integrating into the whole.

In September 2011 I embarked on a project exploring the Future of Western Civilization to create a resource of interviews with visionary leaders at the evolutionary edge of our culture who can share their stories, experiences and inspirational vision is for the future. The aim is to play my part in rejuvenating the self-confidence and direction of our Civilization.

Unleashing Human Potential

Alignment, Energetics and Connection

Soleira Green interviewed by Dr Nicholas Beecroft

Soleira Green is a global visionary and co-founder of the Visionary Network. She is an expert in unleashing human potential, helping people to align with their highest purpose and super connecting to consciousness. She works with individuals, groups and businesses as a trainer, coach, speaker and event host. Soleira has written 15 books including Living Consciousness, New Visionaries, The Alchemical Coach and the Evolution of Everything. Many people talk about these subjects but Soleira and her colleagues have distilled a great deal of practical wisdom into simple how-to guides, manuals and tools.

In this interview Soleira describes her highest vision for the future of Western and global civilization. She believes that we are on an inevitable path to becoming one global civilization; interconnected and vibrant. She sees lots of evidence that people are increasingly choosing to unleash their own full potential and that this works the best when they are in service of the highest collective goals. This is happening across all generations globally and particularly so amongst the young. She describes how we can avoid the sources of resistance and frustration both internal and external. She believes that our energy is best spent not in resisting those things we dislike or in fighting existing structures but rather by letting them be and creating better structures, better ideas and successful ventures which then allow the old problems to fall away. She discusses how this might apply to individuals who currently feel powerless or trapped inside old-fashioned systems.

Soleira describes how we can access different states of consciousness. She believes that our consciousness is connected, in fact, super-connected to a wider consciousness shared with others right from the interpersonal space to the cosmic level. She works with companies and other organizations to optimize the different aspects of their consciousness to help credit fields within which everyone can align in service of their personal and higher goals. She discusses how this may apply to individuals, healthcare, the financial system and education.

Nicholas: Soleira-Green welcome to the series "Exploring the Future of Western Civilization."

Soleira: Thanks Nick. I'm really excited about having this conversation with you.

Nicholas: I've known Soleira for about six years or so now and I can really vouch for her. She is an amazing visionary. She is cofounder of the Visionary Network and I think if you spoke to the many people that know her, they'd all tell you something a bit different, but for me she is an expert in human potential, unleashing human potential, getting people to really align with the highest purpose and mission and creating new ventures, new ideas, new businesses and energizing them, taking them forward. She knows all about sourcing potential, creativeness and vision. She works with individuals one-on-one in training and coaching and she goes around the world teaching large groups of people as a speaker and running events on different subjects.

Today, she is going to share with us many things I'm sure, but starting off with her highest vision for Western and Global Civilization. She is no doubt going to give us some of the tools that she uses along the way. Welcome Soleira.

Soleira: Thank you Nick. I'm so excited about this conversation. It is one of my favorites actually, of building Civilization and what does that look like. It is not something I thought I would be working on in my life but oh my God, does it ever seek me? I just love it.

Nicholas: I know you are the sort of person who likes to jump in at the deep end, so what is your very highest vision for Western or Global Civilization?

Soleira: It is funny, a lot of people when asked that question, bring up immediately bring up the concept of peace and a peaceful world. For me actually it is something other than that. I think that one of the outcomes what I envisioned for the world is that we would all get along but I don't see it as a peaceful world. I see it as a thriving, dynamic highly creative super inventive really enriching world with mega creations, leaps in technology, in science, in education, in abilities. I think those leaps are going to come from accessing our connection to Energy with a capital E and Consciousness with a capital C. the ability to go beyond ourselves to live into the more that which is just waiting to be seeded by us. Sometimes I think that's our role. Our role is to get the more into play. That's been my work.

I started it by getting people to fulfill their potential, to take on their biggest work as you said their greater purpose, etc. At one level I could say that the point why I'm here is to get the big players to be playing in the big game. Everybody else gets to do their work and I get them all together doing theirs together, but also unleashing the unique power of each person's contribution. That is something that's quite different. A lot of people bandy around the term potential. We hear a lot in the coaching profession and that kind of thing. Sometimes I think I may be talking about another layer of that. Not just what we have as inherent potential waiting for us to be better leaders, better coaches, better business people. I'm talking about the access to greatness. The access to legacy; the access to creating a world beyond our imagining because I think the human race has this enormous potential to be something we just can't even envision yet. I strive for that in everything I do every day. I'm working towards the fulfillment of that hopefully in my lifetime although, I have to say, I'm seeing it.

When I started 16 years ago, I wasn't seeing it around us. Even when I started, I think it was 1999, I ran the first conference at that time on leadership and management and of the visionary business and corporate soul and all those kinds of things and new way of doing business and business contributing to the world we didn't see it so much then. There were people on the leading edge and we were all struggling to find our way, to find new language, but if you look today, it is all those players who are real true visionaries creating. You see it showing up in our lives in amazing, practical, powerful, sustainable ways now. I'm really excited about it.

Nicholas: Human beings have always been creative, appropriate to the way they live in their situation. What are you saying is different now, what's changing?

Soleira: There are some people who have lived creative lives and created genius things. Our relationships to genius and creation had been, "Oh they are born with it and oh there is so few who can do that and the rest of us are going to live our normal mundane lives. We will be lucky to have a good, successful career." I think that's turned upside down today. I think now the view for me is that every single person has a unique genius capacity within them that needs to get unleashed and expressed in a creative fashion that if that's done and if it's done with every single person, you will have a collective creativity and genius that we haven't seen before.

Nicholas: How would you tap into that potential or how does someone who is reading this do that?

Soleira: The first thing is you have to get people to unleash themselves and actually I'm finding that that's taking less and less time and less and less efforts. People are more and more ready for that but in years past, we lived in society especially in Western society which is very psychologically based in which people are fairly contained. You are glued to your work and you try to fit into the management mould or you go into the school and you try and get all A's because this is what you are supposed to do and these are the right answers to the test. Do you know what I mean? I'm talking about something different from that. There is an unleashing that's happening in people. It is a kind of natural thing. It is who we were as children. You know when you were kids and you are just running around and you are just doing the do and you are creating like crazy and it is just pouring out of you it is kind of like getting adults or at any age basically to unleash that which is naturally wildly inside of them that wants to come out, that wants to get expressed. That's where our true power is; that's where our passion is; it is where our creativity surges from; it is where a lot of the unique genius pops from. It is that job of getting us to be uncontained. I just finished call with my friend Dorothy who you know and she said, "Unbounded limitless creation."

Now lot of people will say, "Well that's a dream. How do you live inside that every single moment of your day? Can you?" Yes. We can. I think all those people who are like really contained at work, really stiff and limited by how they think they are supposed to be and what their bosses told them they should be and all that kind of thing, I actually find that once they are naturally unleashed everything goes right with that stuff. I don't think we are looking for prescriptive leaders who look like every other leader. I think what's happening is this upsurge of new visionaries around the planet who are creating extraordinarily, ingeniously. Things we haven't even thought of before. They are coming out with it from little tiny villages in Africa and kids on the streets and 75 year old women and it is coming out of the most extraordinary places. No longer are we waiting for the leaders at the top of the society and companies and politics to solve the problems. I think we've all just given up on that. Won't it be nice when they do that too? I think the real power of leadership and creativity and genius is coming out of real deal people who are just getting on with it now.

Nicholas: Presumably it will be a good idea to teach that in schools and transform the way we do education. Have you seen that in action?

Soleira: Yes and no. I think minimally in action in a few ways. Some friends of mine are doing a Youth Brilliance Project right now. I've seen the One Young World which was world leadership by young people around the world. Just look at the you see the stuff in the videos that are coming out of kids themselves, you do see the that the education system is stuck in the twentieth century. What you've got is kids being born and who are evolution of the species. They have abilities that are profoundly beyond what we had as kids. We have those abilities too now. I'm not saying they have something we don't. I think we all are evolving into it. These kids are being born into that genius connection and you can see that. You watch it on the reality TV shows where kids are shown with these enormous talents and the things they are writing, in the way they are inspiring us. It is just quite amazing actually. The education system is being dragged into the Twenty-first Century and not doing a very good job of it in my books.

I will tell you fundamentally why I think that it is. It is still founded upon a mental model of intelligence. We are no longer operating in a mental model of intelligence. We are operating in a super-connected consciousness level of intelligence in which the knowing is streaming to us all the time. Some people will call it vision, I would call it streaming knowing. It is like variation of the language I guess but I actually mean it on that level as well. It is going to take the school system to get moving from the normal mode, everybody fits into the norm to uniqueness, celebrating genius, celebrating passion and working from streaming knowing you need something radical that's got to take place in the education system.

Nicholas: You are talking about something different to our traditional idea of intuition; we've got our intelligence, we've got our heart, our gut we're a separate individual with capacities. You are saying there's something that flows in the space between us that we can access.

Soleira: Absolutely yes. The consciousness. It is a living, breathing, pulsing, space now and we are not separate from that space. We are separate from one another. We are all ridiculously connected at the moment and all I have to do is have that tiny little millisecond thought and you want to try to pull it back. That person emails or calls me immediately. It is just freaky, wonderfully freaky. I love it. What we are creating, we are creating the super-connected us.

Nicholas: I've made the same observation that you have but many of the so-called millennial generation, the youngest group, really are pretty amazing and the stuff that has taken me years to work out, they've got it instantly. That seems to be accelerating. What's the role of those of us who are older than that? Do we just get out of the way or do we have a role in leading it or facilitating it?

Soleira: Oh yeah! I'm sixty-two and I'm not getting out of the way. For me, I think we have a big role to play and part of that role for us, for me especially and all the people I work with, is constantly being willing to source something brand new. I don't think any more in society we can hang on to anything as to how it is even yesterday. Our work or my work simply is constantly changing. The whole marketing concept of branding is out the window for somebody is constantly reinventing what is available and what's being presented, which has its own set of frustrations but at the same time it has its own type of excitement and possibility in it. I couldn't do it any other way. I think the kids and us are all connected to the streaming knowing of full connected consciousness now. In that streaming knowing everything is just as available to you and me as it is to the kids. I think as adults we had more of a job to unlearn what we've been trained in. The kids are coming in pure ...

Nicholas: How can someone tap into that?

Soleira: You have to connect. I will give you an example of the exercises that I would use. If I'm disconnected, okay, I'm all closed up in myself I'm disconnected. Right, (Soleira breathes in and out, closes her eyes, doing something internally) you can see it like bang there I'm Me and my soul here as an isolated individual being and whatever I think and feel doesn't matter because nobody else can know but me I'm inside that. Or, I'm going to give you a couple of levels of it. (Again, Soleira breathes in and out, closes her eyes, doing something internally) I can be available. I can connected and be available to be with you.

Nicholas: What have you done internally to make that happen?

Soleira: I was just relaxed and opened and made myself available to you and to people who are reading and to the world and to life. I just opened up to be available. That's what I call connection. Superconnection is another level of that. Superconnection is (Soleira breathes in and out, closes her eyes, does something internally) Bang. I'm part of the streaming flow of life everywhere. I'm part of the cosmos pulsing itself into creation. I'm the ability to be anything I chose to be in this moment because I have access to all possibility.

Nicholas: Again what have you done internally to do that, how did you do that?

Soleira: I've taken every cell of me and connected it to every cell of everything everywhere. The space between us is rich and full with life, with consciousness, with energy, with possibility and I have simply made myself that. It is not the oneness piece. I'm not trying to be one with everything. If I go be one with everything, I kind of lose my uniqueness but if I become the unique totality expressing itself, wow, now I've got access to limitless energy. I've got to access to the flow of genius. I've got access to possibilities I wouldn't have considered before. Everything is available to me to live my life from in a very brilliant, magical kind of way.

Nicholas: When you were speaking earlier, you were saying that I think you read out our friend Dorothy's words, what did you say?

Soleira: "Unbounded limitless creations."

Nicholas: Yes, who could say that wasn't wonderful and as you then immediately alluded to that someone might say that sounds really unrealistic. I was talking last week in one of these interviews to a really lovely doctor who is very inspiring, very caring, and he has been really on a 15-year mission in New Zealand and more recently globally to try to inspire people to really compassionate and integrated healthcare. He said that he was reflecting on his experience really and he said that at the end of 15 years, he was really tired of smacking his head against the wall, trying to persuade people; trying to evolve the existing structures. He said he had just given up on that. In my experience that's true as well. Lots of our organizations, whether it is the health service or education or many big businesses and so on, lots of people find themselves strapped in by particular styles of leadership roles and so on, what's your advice to them to really unleash the potential?

Soleira: I've got some great advice for that one. Step away from trying to fix what is, slide around it and create something new. As long as you are trying to fix what is, it grips on and so your journey is hard. If you just leave it alone, give it no energy, it will dissolve in time, so you slip around it and you create the new thing that you are passionate about. You call to all the players who want to create it new with you and that way you are not tired. You are refreshed and vital and visionary and energized and energizing.

Nicholas: To me that is practical for some people who are in the kind of roles where they can easily do that but many people can't just leave and set up something new. This morning I was talking to a doctor in the National Health Service who is really burnt out from trying to do their job in that system. Obviously you could say well just leave and create your own practice or but that's not realistic for everybody. The NHS dominates the medical system. How can somebody having to work without this within that framework do what you are saying?

Soleira: If I took your example of the doctor you are speaking about right now, my guess is that he has to orient himself to what's really true and right for him. I would ask questions why did he become a doctor in the first place and is that being fulfilled by him now through his existing practice? Healthcare, in my books, is making us sicker not better but what is making us better are all of those things where somebody is creating new possibilities.

For a doctor like that he could stay in there and simply orient to what is right and true for him which might be, "I'm going to stay and do the things that make people well." Sometimes it might be but mostly I don't think it is. There is a different way, there is a different approach. So he could find, inside the system, he could find his own way to make that right for himself, so he would feel fulfilled at the end of the day that he was making a difference. He might have to see less people. He might have to make less money that's a possibility so I don't know whether that would work for him or not but what I found with most people who are frustrated and exhausted, the greater part of their being that is directing their life is getting them to realize that this is a dead end. It doesn't work anymore. The system is defunct. It doesn't work. Trying to push at it and fix it simply makes you more tired. The only way I can see through that is to step out and around and create that which does work.

That doesn't mean you can't make as much money, so in a doctor's case what if he became one of the new breed of doctors who is saying, "I'm going to source you well through nutrition; through exercise; through proper things to true wellness, I'm going to do that for you. I'm going to build the practice around that." He could do that. I don't know what would happen legally and I don't know what would happen pharmaceutically because they exert a lot of pressures on doctors like that and probably he has got a big house; he has got a family and he has got all those things to be concerned about. That's the big trap for a lot of people. I get that but at the same point, when your being is pressing you and you are exhausted, the only option inside there you don't handle it in some way is to get sick and probably leave the planet soon. That's not what they are meant to be doing. These are big players. They are meant to be creating the new. It is just they are being pushing in that direction.

Nicholas: If you look at the group level and ask what is the state of the world, what one lens to look through is that it is amazing. There are all these incredible things going on, evolution at incredible speed like never before and that's true but also many people, myself included, can look through the negative lens. If you read the Daily Mail it will say, "Oh there's terrible crime. Immigration is out of control. People are sponging off the welfare state. There are riots everywhere." Or you can read the Guardian and it will say, "It is terrible, global warming. There is inequality in the world. There is so much injustice and so on." The thing is all those things are true.

Soleira: Well, are they? It is not true just because the newspapers says it is by the way.

Nicholas: I think in my view it is valid to look at things in that way but it seems to be a dead end because it makes you angry, upset, and powerless and you feel like it is just too much. If someone is stuck in that state looking at those things which are real threats, real issues real problems, how do you then turn that round.

Soleira: First of all, there are a million ways to look at anything. I don't believe there is a truth anywhere. I've stopped looking for the truth. I think no matter what you look at there are 50 million ways to see it. For example, global climate change. Is that true? There is some question as to whether that's actually true today. You could say there is lot of scientific evidence for it and didn't Al Gore do this great documentary but, equally valid today, there's a real question as to whether that's true. I, for example, got an email this morning from NASA, I get their updates, saying that scientists had just found that under ice plankton blooms which is the equivalent of finding a flowering field in the middle of the desert. It's impossible. What they are finding at the moment it is impossible. Here is this thriving life going on under the ice that's melting which is supposed to be tragic.

Another example like I was just home on the St Lawrence River in Ontario I noticed how clean it was and it has been polluted for years where I lived anyway because there's chemical plant that's nearby. My brother who worked for the coast guard said, "We had an infestation of European mollusks" or something like that, one of those things that latch onto boats. He said they said they went crazy, ate up all the pollution and then they just all disappeared. The water is clean. "Something is happening" so that we had better keep our our lens, as you call, it on the right focus. Wherever you put your focus is what grows.

The media would have us keep our focus on all the things that are wrong because they think that's what sells papers. The truth is that if you keep your focus on what's brilliantly emerging it is a whole different world. It is a creational world full of promise and brilliance and amazing things. There are miracles happening in nature right now and I'm just saying this couple I just mentioned are extraordinary and there is going to be more of that we are going to see in the next little while because I think we just stepped into the miraculous millennium. That's where I think we are and I think everything is going to go off the charts. We can't imagine or predict right now what it is going to be like even next year. It is really amazing totally.

The more we keep our energy and focus on that the more that grows. I recommend to people that stop and pay attention to that crazy stuff. Let the banks go. I can hear people gasping as I say that, blahblahblah, but you know what? The banking system was probably meant to fail 3 or 4 years ago when they did all the bailouts around the world. Wouldn't it be nice if they had I think but look what's replacing it? Peer-to-peer lending websites. Oh my gosh, that's amazing. Microfinance opportunities for entrepreneurs. Amazing new stuff that's again coming from the power of the people, sharing, creating, collaborating together. It is not the big business era anymore. We haven't quite lost it yet because people still think that's where it is but that's not really where it is going to be. We are going to in a global collective era. It is a global society and we are already seeing businesses who are starting to be really good businesses are ones who are contributing to making that global society a better place to be in. Innocent Smoothies of course is my favorite example ever of a company doing that and of course our own business, the Visionary Network and others that we are seeing. There's dozens where ten years ago I could barely pick together an example of a company like that and now they are thriving and we're seeing loads of them.

Nicholas: As you are talking, I'm hearing you say it is inevitable that we are moving towards a global Civilization in which we are all interconnected and actually within that we are all kind of conscious cells or parts, each of which is independent and connected to the whole. When each person taps into their own mission in alignment with the highest goals that's when the energy really kicks in and that's when things really work.

Soleira: Yes absolutely that's when it really works. You see people unleashed irresistibly unleashed. There is a real attractiveness to people who are unleashed. Do you know what I mean? They are free flowing and fun to be with. They are coming up with new ideas all the time. They have great energy and great vitality and that's what I think we are going to start seeing our global society be and people contributing to that global society in either way. Kids, they are already connected all over the world just by the internet and social media and Facebook and stuff like that. When I was a kid, in 1950, that was a long time ago, by the time I was 18 I'd never gone more than 60 miles away from tiny little town that I grew up in. I had no access. I had never even seen a black person for example. My first one was when I was 18. Oh my God that was wonderful for me because I had no perceptions of it. I was like, "Well look, even we looked differently." I thought it was fabulous.

Today I have friends who have kids who at the age of 14 have probably been in 20 countries. It is very different today. The globality of us is extraordinary now. Let me also talk about cosmic aspects and make that practical because we are being inundated by cosmic images and cosmic energy at the moment. We are right on the cusp of realizing that we are not just an isolated world and I'm not talking about spacious land and or any of that stuff. That's not what I mean. I mean that we are becoming aware of our part in a thriving galaxy; in a thriving universe. In ways that weren't even possible before 1996 and Hubble telescope. When I grew up, space is a cold empty dark space and those men walking on the moon when I was a teenager, "Oh my God, that was a big deal." Now we are just being swamped by the day with breathtaking images and the science is evolving so fast because of what the telescopes are finding and receiving. That has to alter our framework of how we perceive ourselves as an isolated world. I think we are going to be superconnected cosmically as well, whatever that's going to look like, whether we find there's other planets for life; whether we just simply understand our place in the cosmos I don't know but I'm excited by that possibility as well.

Nicholas: Yes, if what you are saying is true that consciousness extends not just outside of our body but between us and then into space, then presumably it would be pretty amazing if there weren't other life forms and Civilizations in the cosmos. Presumably somehow it might be possible for us at some stage to connect with that.

Soleira: I think so. I do think right now technology would look at putting ourselves in a spaceship and shooting ourselves across light years but I think that technology is going to evolve very quickly and in this century where I think you are going to open a portal and step through and be somewhere else. The Stargates and all that stuff you watched in TV I think that's creating a space in the consciousness for the possibility of that to be real. There's probably people working on it today, that would be my guess. We may not be hearing about it but I bet it's being worked on. Why would it not? It's the frontier of science. That's the exciting stuff. So I do think that's coming.

Even ourselves in consciousness, I know I can literally take myself to journey anywhere I want now. I'm not talking about taking my physical body and teleporting it although I think that's coming too and very quickly. One of these kids will show up and do it and that will be just in the consciousness and the rest of us will go, "Oh, okay that's who you do it." We just don't believe it yet but I do believe it's coming. It is not something I'm particularly focussed on. I'm working on the superconnection of us and the evolution of us as a species to become something geniusly brilliant that we weren't going to become anyway if we didn't get to work on it. That's me.

Nicholas: Some people think that we are connected through fields, lots of separate beings within a system whether the physical system or the organization or family or the whole planet, there is some kind of conscious field within which we align. How do we make that practical? For example, if someone has a new business venture or if someone is running a Police Service or an Army Regiment or something, how do you create the conscious fields within which everyone aligns for the highest purpose?

Soleira: Beautiful! That's a whopper question. There are three ways of relating to consciousness, well maybe four. If you include four is, there isn't any. Some people think there isn't any. It is just empty dead space. One level would be consciousness at the dead static space that holds information. You just go to it and you get information. When I first started working with consciousness 20 years ago that I went higher to get information and brought it back. It was like a library. Another way of relating to consciousness is as an energy field, vibrant, vital dynamic energy fields which are creational in which you can source them, you can manage them. You can create them. You can accelerate them. You can connect them, move them around. Kind of like Lego. If you want to take a simple application of it, you can create fields.

The last way of looking at consciousness is that there is a thriving, pulsing, sentient presence as the cosmos itself that you and I are part of, not only a part of but can be the whole of as well. We can both part of and the whole of it simultaneously. Having a relationship with consciousness as a pulsing force of creation with sentient knowledge and ability allows for me and anybody who takes it on to reach something far beyond what you could consider in the other levels. I think to answer the question you asked practically, I'm going to step into that middle level which is creational fields.

In a business that I've done this with people, if you take any business it already has an existing field of consciousness and energy. Even if it is a brand new business just starting as a single owner or person, the more they work with it, the more the business becomes a field of its own and you can actually work with that field to grow it, to tune into it, to see what it wants and just like tending a garden. You can grow the field of your business and make it into something more. I can also for any business tune into it on the variety of levels of consciousness and fields to see what's going on. Any business

25

will have its people, its visions, its potentiality, its weighted problems, its customers, all different aspects of the energy that you can take as a part and work with each one differently. I'm gave the example in the book I wrote few years ago of McDonalds. This was in 2002. I tuned into McDonalds potential at that time as to what it could be and I saw that it could be leading nutritional fast food market and if they did that, it would just revolutionize McDonalds role in the world. No, they didn't do that. As a result, they spent billions on lawsuits and Supersize Me films had put them down and people were criticizing them about how they dealt with animals and what it is doing to your body to eat that kind of food. Now they are lagging behind everybody else on the nutritional stuff. They could have been leaders in the field in 2002.

That within the field of the business. You don't have to be a strategist to figure that out although I'm a strategist I did do that on a business in a big company years ago, but you just have to tune into the energy. The energy will tell you what its next potential is.

Nicholas: To be really contemporary here, the Euro is unraveling and every day there is a new ridiculous bailout putting off the collapse for a few more days. What's our potential currency wise, financial system wise, what's the positive possibility on the other side of that?

Soleira: I think the whole basis of our financial system is again based on an erroneous foundation-profit at any cost. That's what finance and business is based on. I'm all for everybody making good money but not at any cost. I think that's got to get bounced out here. The banks at the moment are charging 34% interest on your credit card which is just ludicrous. I'm glad we had credit cards. It gave us a huge swing at abundance in the past years. I think everything that has given us good potential but I think that's used up. I think we've now got to find along with the global connection, global community, along with businesses orienting to true purpose and real contribution. I think we have to find a finance system that works with all that such as these peer-to-peer lending, microfinance, whatever else we are coming up with today, something like Kickstarter, there is another one where you go on and get funding in your own creational ways through many investors. Those are some of the other ways that are emerging right now.

It is putting it back right again and that needs to happen. I'm not one of those people with a million pounds in the bank somewhere so I'm not concerned about the banks failing. I'm fortunate in that respect I would say, but I think it's just got to get right. One of the other things I have seen recently on the internet is people giving money to people in need. I think even the whole thing with charity needs to be revolutionized. Charities, some of them did some good work, but they become organizational entities in themselves that are now eating up money with these huge massive organizations, so very little ends up in the hand of the people who actually need it.

I saw this whole thing on the internet about some store like, it wasn't KMart or Target, but someone like that was closing US and these people were standing in line having to pay bills. It was Christmas and somebody just came up and paid every single person's bill because they had extra money and they wanted to help out. People are starting to do things like that. In the microfinance industry Kiva.org which is based in States but works with hundreds of countries as far as I'm aware. They just started a pilot called Kiva Detroit where they've taken five social organizations and let the people of Detroit put money into microfinance. It is being given to people in the poor areas in Detroit to start their own businesses, to be trained and then to have these five community support groups make sure that the businesses are supported locally to grow. That's the way it is going to work. It is not some big banker deciding whether or not you get the investment. It is real people investing in real people. Kiva has a **98.8%** payback on all of their loans. Isn't that amazing?

Nicholas: Yes.

Soleira: Even in the peer-to-peer lending I was just reading something on that. My gosh, almost everybody gets their money back, the investment comes back with interest.

Nicholas: That's not what people would expect.

Soleira: No but it is what's true when we really truly connect and do what's right.

Nicholas: The kind of shifts in consciousness and the evolutionary potential that you are talking about, I've witnessed that myself. There is no question that it is a global phenomenon and that you can see in the Arab spring or just traveling around the world. I've met people from all sorts of countries who are doing what you are talking about, but my sense is that the speed of it and the pace of it is fastest in the Western countries and the most advanced countries. Just as we've got lots of really old backward structures with old beliefs and things that are not working anymore that's absolutely true of the rest of the countries but of course they are getting more and more powerful. Is it possible that these new shoots of a global consciousness will be cut off at the base if, say, the Chinese become very imperialistic or if the Islamic fundamentalists win and manage to create a massive Caliphate and take us back to all the darker, less enlightened consciousness, is it inevitable that this is going to have a happy outcome?

Soleira: Absolutely. I will tell you why. Because it is surging up to every single person on the planet. One of the things I see today in any of the groups that I work with is this burning desire to make a difference. If they are contained in jobs where they are doing that that burning desire is eating at them like crazy. No matter who does what you will not stamp out that emerging fire in people to create, to be global, to work around everything. I don't think even if some system tried to impose it, I don't think it could kill it now. It is too alive in people everywhere. The new kids, oh my God, they are just being born into it. How could you conceive a world with those kids in charge that would be anything but amazing?

I do think if we watched the news and we would think that 90% of the world is in trouble, but you know what? It isn't. It is only a small percentage of the world that's actually in trouble. The average person is doing great.

Nicholas: Syria is currently in the awful beginning stages of a civil war but of course the reason that they are in that difficult situation is precisely because people are waking up and demanding and wanting higher, better form of consciousness and that's a challenge.

Soleira: I can't talk about that specifically, I'm not familiar enough with it, but I do think any country where you've got that kind of pulsing, what shows up in warfare or conflict, those are newly emerging countries. It is showing up in conflict because there is so much energy, there is so much possibility, there is so much newness coming through. I think what we are probably starting to see now is that once that is through, it starts to show up differently. I have seen some stuff recently about things going on in Africa and things like that there were countries that were just like, Oh my gosh, the most atrociously violent things happening where suddenly now you are seeing the rebuilding of society coming up fresh and new and different out of that. I don't believe the conflict or tragedy is how we have to achieve our potential. In fact it is one of the big things that I'm about. We can achieve our potential in super conscious grace that if we know what it is that we can reach to it and fulfill it without any conflict without any challenges or problems and make it work for everybody.

I've been calling the new visionaries winnovators so they create win, win, win for everybody and I believe that is a new thinking that looks from there, that creates from there. No one loses in that game. The old paradigm business and finance and education model is more founded on winners and losers. That's just not the new model. It is just not how it is going to work for us.

Nicholas: Soleira, earlier I asked you about how we do with external resistance. When someone finds themselves apparently tied in by all existing structures, but of course, I know from my personal experience and also my experience as a psychiatrist that we experience massive internal resistance. That's probably actually bigger than the external. For example, a classic would be that I would say or I would be love be super fit and slim and eat much better and of course that doesn't necessarily work out because we have different parts of ourselves pulling in different directions. We have low moods, we have wounds, we have negativity, we have primitive impulses and dark parts of ourselves that are not processed. How do you advise people to do in order to reach their highest potential?

Soleira: I have a kind of different view, a different come-from place about all that. I would say to people first of all, please believe there is

29

nothing wrong with you. That's the first thing. A lot of our psychological orientation in Western society would have us look inward to see what's wrong, a lot, so we are constantly reflecting the outer circumference with an inward journey of seeing what's wrong. I think that too has had value. I think we've maybe past the value point with that one. I think it's now got us as a trap. No matter what happens externally we look inward to see what's wrong. First I'm going to say there is nothing wrong with you.

Second I would say, learn to live energetically in flow and that means you have to tend yourself energetically for a little while until it becomes a natural state. It is a natural state for us to be vibrant, vital, dynamic, and creative but people are so not used to that. You have to be aware and kind of regiment yourself just a little bit into living in what I call the high-vibe, the higher vibrational frequencies where all the good stuff is happening. It could be as simple as if you are feeling down, you just take a deep breath (breathes in) think of something you love, imagine you are skiing down a slope or standing on a beach or looking out to the garden and see the sun, listen to the birds sing. It could be as simple as that. It raises your frequency to a better place. When you think of something you love, it exhilarates the energy in you. There's those two things.

The third thing would be always seek to create the next new. The resistance we experience is trained into us because we think we are supposed to stay in the same job for the whole of life. We are supposed to..A...B...C...all those big stresses in life are supposed to be things that we are not supposed to achieve. You don't move countries; you don't move house; you don't change your jobs. That's just ridiculous in today's world. You can have six to seven jobs in your lifetime now. We might still embrace it and enjoy and revel in it. Go seek the thrill of that.

One of the things that I'm finding people that I've worked with and that's quite a number in the last 20 years, they've stepped away from the traditional world somewhat and have learned to trust that life will turn out if you get in the right place with it. They are not so terrified by, "Oh my God. I lost my job. How am I going to eat?" It is more of an adventure for them and I think those people have done a big piece of work in consciousness to put into the planet that we are on an adventure and it is going to be okay. I haven't seen any of my people I know go starve or be homeless yet not at all, some of them, I've gotten one friend of mine who is just doing the most amazing stuff. She just came back from the deserts in Egypt and she is being a groupie following bands around and just living her life in the pure magical joy of what she wants to do and, oh my gosh, who would've thought you could live like that. That as an extraordinary contribution as somebody who is working on the top of a company making big company, in my books. There is a kind of reorienting of our come-from place with it all.

Nicholas: The last thing I wanted to ask you was, actually about this project that I'm doing what I've called so far the Exploring the Future of Western Civilization. What is the potential for that project and beyond?

Soleira: I do think you are opening up the possibility of conversations for what we can become and I think that needs to happen. I don't think there is enough of that going on. Great visionary conversations about what's possible now and what really is happening and how come we look at that differently, how can we shape it? There is also the beautiful potential of bringing together all those people who are creating something like the doctor you talked about who you interviewed last week who is hitting his head against the wall. There is a value when you stand with other visionaries, when you speak with them, when you hang out with them, it strengthens something in you. It helps to provide great direction and you're putting a focus on it, you are putting energy to it, you are building conversation to possibility and you are creating network of support to those people who are creating those networks and I think that's just brilliant. Bravo!

Nicholas: Thank you Soleira. Before we finish, is there anything that you'd like to add?

Soleira: Again, while there is a world going on that's a little bit in turmoil and dissolution, there is a world going on that's in pure creation, in real excited adventure into what's possible in the Twenty-first century. I think this world is starting to take predominance now in 2012 over that other world. Hallelujah. We've been talking about it for 16 years, so now

I think we are there. I think we are about to see something. I don't know what it is, not a quite prediction but something is going to happen which is going to be so visible that the world is there now that nobody will doubt that that now world now has prominence.

Nicholas: Thank you so much Soleria. Absolutely fantastic.

Soleira: Wonderful.

Nicholas: For anyone who would like to follow you work, see what you've been up to, comes to one of your courses, may contact, what contact do you recommend?

Soleira: It's our website www.transformingourworld.com is the best place to connect with me. I also have http://www.soleiragreen.com they can connect with me through there but most of our current work and offerings on www.transformingourworld.com.

Nicholas: Thank you very much.

Soleira: Thank you.

Nicholas: Bye.

Wise Democracy

Discovering Solutions to Intractable Problems

Jim Rough interviewed by Dr Nicholas Beecroft

Jim Rough is an expert in Wise Democracy. He originated the technique called dynamic facilitation which he now uses with Wisdom Councils, a social process designed to empower large systems of people. In this interview Jim describes how the quality of conversation which really counts along with the people who have that conversation. Dynamic facilitation takes people beyond the traditional debate, dialogue and deliberation into a choice-creating conversation which generates new potential outcomes. The groups work best when drawn randomly from the population. On first inspection that may sound strange because our tradition is to choose experts, representatives and those who have a particular strong opinion or interest group. With years of experience in facilitating the democratic process, Jim has found that there is a deep wisdom which emerges from randomly chosen group taking the mainstream interest and seeking to serve the whole. He finds that a consensus emerges which is often transformational and inspiring to the wider community. He has taught people globally to use this technique any give some examples of work is working well, particularly in Austria.

We tend to take democracy for granted is as if it is something which we have already achieved. Jim points out that democracy is something which needs constant evolution, requiring ongoing attention and adaptation to our needs and situation. He makes a powerful call for integrating dynamic facilitation and Wisdom Councils into our existing structures so as to help raise our game to meet the substantial challenges which we face.

Jim is a business consultant, speaker, and principal seminar leader for the seminar Dynamic Facilitation and the Wisdom Council. He has been leading public seminars on Dynamic Facilitation for over 20 years, while facilitating for clients that include government agencies, corporations, and community-based organizations. He is author of the book "Society's

33

Breakthrough! Releasing Essential Wisdom and Virtue in All the People", which Robert E. Steele called, "...certainly one of the hundred most important books available in English." He is originator of the Wisdom Council process, which is now being implemented in many cities throughout Central Europe, government agencies, cooperatively owned businesses, schools, and communities. He is cofounder of the nonprofit Center for Wise Democracy, which promotes the Wisdom Council.

Nicholas: Jim Rough, welcome to the series Exploring the Future of Western Civilization.

Jim: I'm glad to be here, Nicholas.

Nicholas: For anyone that hasn't met Jim, Jim is a consultant, an author, and a speaker in social innovation. He originated a technique called Dynamic Facilitation which he has taught all over the world. He originated a process called the Wisdom Council which is the way to empower large systems of people, a technology for democracy which is now being used in cities, states, organizations all around the world. He's written several books including Society's Breakthrough releasing the essential wisdom and virtue of all the people and he is cofounder of the nonprofit Center for Wise Democracy. For eight years he hosted the Jim Rough Show. We're here really today to talk about the future of democracy. Jim, welcome.

Jim: Glad to be here, Nicholas.

Nicholas: When I've asked a lot of people what's important to you about Western Civilization or what makes you proud to be British or American, etc, one of the first things that rolls off people's tongues is freedom and democracy. It's one of those things that we can take for granted. What actually is democracy?

Jim: Democracy should be demos-cracy; the word means the common people and power to the common people. The real meaning of the word is something about we the people being ultimately in charge.

Nicholas: What's the state of health of democracy currently?

34

Jim: We never really had a democracy. I think there were flashes but we have a republic in which the word breaks out to be respublica which is a thing of the people. Basically it means that somewhere in our history there was this agreement that was made that was supposedly be of service to the people and we all supposedly agreed to it; to a social contract. The state of ours is horrible frankly. The state of our republic in my mind, of course I'm an American and I think in terms of the US Constitution.

I think that the situation was beautifully designed and at one point in time. In the US there was a marvelous founding moment where they think the rest of the world really has based their idea of democracy was what the word, they call it and on that founding moment, I think, and of course the history of Great Britain and the Magna Carta and all that. I don't think it can make it. I don't think it's possible to design a system and set it up, turn it loose then have it be in charge of us for 230 years or more and not have problems.

Nicholas: What are you saying? The original operating system wasn't quite right or it's gone awry or it's not suited to current circumstances?

Jim: It was beautifully designed for its time but times have changed since then. Our current system is designed as a competition between special interests. One of the great innovations was that it supposedly took all that power and decision making and put it on the table so anybody could see what was happening. To take the ordinary motivations of people and direct them towards serving the whole and it did that very well, I think, for a long time. The problem is that we now are interdependent and increasingly interdependent. We used to be independent.

The system was designed for us to be independent. It's like a game, a competition between special interests. Now we're interdependent and the game no longer works. It's breaking down. We're trashing the planet. We're destroying our own people.

Nicholas: If we flip to the other end of the spectrum, what's your highest vision for Western or Global Civilization in terms of democracy?

Jim: I have a solution strategy. I'm very very optimistic because I think this solution strategy is a slam dunk. I think it's going to happen, that it's inevitable, and basically the solution is that we need to have a way that all us can be in conversation and have that where we're trying to find what's best for everybody and where that conversation really is the ultimate authority in society. Once we have that conversation, once all of us call time out and step aside and say how are we doing and is this what we want and what would you like to see and let's be clever here and figure out what works for you and me.

Once we have that conversation in play then we have something approximating to a true democracy. I call it a wise democracy. That's where the conversation of all of us is thoughtful, respectful, creative conversation is the ultimate authority.

Nicholas: Why is there any need to improve on what we've got already because some people might say we've got a fine democracy now. I was brought up to think that democracy was something which we have achieved, it's now in process and it's now functioning. Is that not correct?

Jim: That's not correct. In fact, in the US, it's worse than that. In the US, if there's ever a problem, most Americans say, "Oh gosh we have to get back to what the founders were thinking." These are people 230 years ago who didn't have automobiles or airplanes or flush toilets, let alone the internet. They didn't have our problems with the environment or anything and yet being designed a great system for themselves. Of course one of the great founders wasn't at the constitutional convention. Thomas Jefferson, he thought that this kind of thinking together where we figure out a constitution would happen about every 19 years because obviously the one working right now can't last that long. That's the way it should be. We should be thinking there should be a we the people conversation happening in the background all the time.

Nicholas: What's the solution strategy?

Jim: I call it the Wisdom Council and I believe it should be a global Wisdom Council. I think there should be a national Wisdom Council for the United States and for Great Britain. I think every city should have one. I think every polity should have a Wisdom Council process. Basically what happens is that once every maybe three times a year, maybe once every four months or more there's a random selection of 12 people. This is happening right away in cities of Austria especially right now and some in Germany and a little bit in Switzerland and there's a lot of noise about it in the UK too.

We've done experiments in Canada and the US also. Basically you randomly select 12 citizens and let's say we take the debt crisis in Greece. We randomly select 12 citizens and they are given this debt crisis. They're facilitated, and this is the key, they're dynamically facilitated to engage in a certain kind of conversation and that conversation is heartfelt and creative and collaborative where they have breakthrough answers that work for everybody. They engage in that conversation for a short time, maybe two days.

Maybe they hear about the situation from experts for a couple of days beforehand and at the end of their short period, and these were just ordinary citizens but they come up with a unanimous story of basically, well here's how we started out, we didn't know anything, we didn't know what we were thinking about, we had these differences of opinions and we had some breakthroughs along the way. We realized that the real problem wasn't the country going bankrupt but the real problem was, how do we enjoy our lives; how do we have our real life; how do we put together the resources of the people and the needs of the people? How do we put those together in the best possible way? Something like that.

Then they would mention their strategy for how to do that which I don't know what it would be but they would come with something or they would come up with the start of something. They present their unanimous perspective back to the country, as many people as we can have involved and as many people as possible paying attention. Then all the Greek citizens would consider this and basically what we found is that when they hear this story and you have a random group like this, they basically say yes, "Let's do that. That's really the way we should be looking at it and that's what we ought to be doing." Even though you have selected unconscious people or stuck people or narrow minded people and also brilliant people and people from the left and people from the right; even though you have this diverse group, they can be facilitated to get into a spirit of thinking and talking where they'd come up with something that's best for everybody and they're all excited about it and they don't notice the process.

They look around the room and think how do we get these people together? How did these people show up in this room? Of course they're random. It's really the process but they're wonderful too. The people are wonderful.

Nicholas: Is that called Dynamic Facilitation?

Jim: Yes.

Nicholas: That's the technology. What does that involve?

Jim: The key is that we set up a system where whatever anybody says is okay. We help people to speak with feelings. Normal meeting processes are, "Hey we don't want you talking about this, we don't want you talking about that, here's what you can talk about, let's put guidelines on the wall so we limit how we speak, let's make sure we don't say anything negative to anybody." Normally we have all these rules and regulations and we try to limit how people think. Then we do our best to separate our feelings. We try and be rational and we try to say, "Hey leave your passions at the door; let's just figure out, let's be rational, let's be deliberative, let's be objective, let's be neutral, let's whatever."

Dynamic Facilitation, the dynamic facilitator, the DFer is responsible for keeping everybody safe but what we want is everybody to just speak their truth and do it however it comes out. No guidelines on the wall, no restrictions. Nobody gives you, "Here's the problem, here are the possible solutions, weigh them." They just give you a mess and you figure out and whatever anybody says, we use 4 charts. Everybody faces the 4 charts. Everybody faces the DFer and the 4 charts encompass the whole possibility of what people might say. One is a set of solutions. One is a set of concerns.

Another is a set of problem statements and a 3rd is a set of data, just data. The DFer holds this space, this perspective on the problem we're working. We're working on a problem and it's messy and it's difficult and it's impossible-seeming. We don't think we can solve it. We're being creative. We're just allowing what you say to come up and we're helping to make sure that at some point it looks like a puzzle, that what everybody says begins to look like we're all together on this and every time somebody says something, it actually helps. We make progress through breakthroughs rather than through linear analysis.

Nicholas: I've been in lots of group settings so I've got a feel for the chemistry of what you're talking about. There's a thousand questions I'd like to ask you really. I think a lot of people are listening would say if you get 12 people together about a topic that they feel quite passionate about, there's going to be a lot of emotional triggering, you get polarization, you get conflict and so on. That can all be dealt with in a really healthy way and productive way. How do you get from that to this amazing visionary consensus? How do you deal with those sparks and those challenges?

Jim: We want the sparks. We encourage that. We want people to say with feeling what their, we call it the purge, what their purge answer is. They're not talking to you. They're talking to the facilitator. The facilitator is really interested and he or she is capturing what they're saying on a chart as a solution strategy for instance. We need to get rid of the bankers and I don't know what they're saying. They're saying the left wing is all the problem or the right wing is all the problem. Whatever it is, we're capturing it as data or as a solution strategy and we're helping that person just empty themselves.

They're putting their whole perspective right there on the wall and everybody listens. They're listening because they're actually talking to the dynamic facilitator and it's being captured and it's being heard and if somebody wants to interrupt, that's okay too. If somebody says, "No that's the stupidest idea I've ever heard," we say, "Can you hold on to what you were saying a minute ago; let's go with this guy for a minute. You have a concern and we reframe it now as a concern. It was a judgment, now it's a concern. Can you tell us what your concern is?" We go over the list of concerns and we capture what that person, really what they're worried about, what they're worried is going to happen.

Then we say what would be an even better idea and when do we capture their solution. Then we go back to the person who is speaking and interrupted and say, "Now we interrupted you, can you keep going?" In other words, we just try and work it out like real people trying to hear one another, trying to figure out what's best for everybody. That's what we're doing here. Trying to hear people and we're trusting that what emerges from people even though in an ordinary meeting, it would be a killer. It would ruin the meeting. We're trusting it. We're saying that came up for some reason. Some intelligence in you is coming up with that and we want to know what it is. We want to hear it. That's the basic idea is we're just taking whatever is bubbling up from people, we're honoring it, and we're beginning to notice after a while that my goodness, all this is fitting together in exciting ways. The energy starts to shift. First of all, we want the energy and then when we've got the energy in the room like that, now we're following it. The energy shifts, we have energy breakthroughs. People go oh my goodness, that isn't even the problem; the real problem is we shouldn't even be in this system; why are we in this system? It's stupid to be in a system where we're going bankrupt and we're the people.

They have insights like that and then they say how do we set up something that would allow us to bring together the resources of people and the needs of people in some way that makes better sense.

Nicholas: Jim, could you give an example. You've been all over the world applying these techniques. Could you give a practical example of somewhere where this has happened and worked really well and had a real impact in the world?

Jim: My favorite example is in the city of Bregenz, Austria which is right on Lake Constance. They have there a beautiful lake, a beautiful park, and then they have a railroad track and then a highway then the city. Right in the heart of the city, right against the highway is a parking lot that's been a parking lot for many years. The reason why it's been a parking lot is because it's the most valuable maybe part of the whole city and they haven't been able to figure out what to do with it because it's too controversial.

Manfried Helrigl who's the Director of The Office of Future Related Issues, I love that title, in Vorarlberg went to the Mayor and said hey if you want to deal with this, possibly we could do a Wisdom Council. They did. They set up a random selection of citizens who met for just a day and a half, that's all, and they met ahead of time with the developer and the Mayor and some experts. Then they closed the door and then they were dynamically facilitated. They came out of the room with a shift, a breakthrough and their shift was gee, this is a 100 year opportunity for us to get what we want and what we want in this city is to be connected to the lake.

The developers had an underpass set up there but they thought what we could do is raise the level of the project so that the project would spill over the highway and the railroad track and down onto the, like a Spanish stairway down to the park and the lake. The developers basically said, "Wow, why didn't we think of that?" They've been working on it 2 years or whatever. The values hadn't been there. Then the Mayor said my God, that's great, that's good. There weren't many people at the event. These projects are just getting started. We don't have the whole community in conversation yet but this was enough just with a few people showing up to avoid the usual conflict and now the project is underway.

Nicholas: Wow. Was that just on one workshop or was that over a period of time?

Jim: It was just one Wisdom Council. The Wisdom Council has 12 principles and one of the principles is that it's ongoing. We have exceptions. We've never really done a real Wisdom Council process because it would transform everything and it scares people. We've done the kind where we give them a topic and we do a limited period of time and it's just a slam dunk. If you're in government, you want to know about this and you want to do this. Here's a way to solve your big problems and involve the citizens and build community at the same time.

Nicholas: Any city anywhere in the world whether it's in Iran, China or the North of England, you have a bunch of people sitting in a room having a conversation about what should we do about how we manage this city or this hospital or how do we run the Police Force in this area or whatever the thing is. There's a bunch of people in a room having a conversation. What's different in the chemistry or the methodology of the Wisdom Council to that?

Jim: Yes, well, that is the key piece.

Nicholas: In other words, why isn't that happening already everywhere currently?

Jim: That's exactly right. If you gather just people in a room, they will have a conversation and then now we need to figure out what's the caliber of that conversation. Is it a dialogue? Is it a deliberation? Is it a negotiation? Is it a debate? Is it some kind of presentation? What is the nature? Is it a discussion? What's the nature of the conversation that we need to have? Let's figure out what the kind of conversation we want is and let's structure for that. What we have in our society today is that our fundamental conversation in what we call a democracy, the ideal is a rational debate. That's the ideal and that's not adequate. That's more fight. That's more battle.

There are people wandering around saying we should compromise. Okay, now we're talking negotiation. Then there are people saying no we really should be deliberative. We should be having deliberative democracy so let's all sit there and weigh these different options that we've been given and see if that, and that usually means a vote at the end. If you randomly select a small group, you end up with 14 in favor and 10 against or something. You don't really have any information there. Then others say let's do a dialogue. Dialogue is a great form of conversation too but you don't end up with any answer. You're just there talking. Maybe you come up with an answer but chances are you don't. In fact nobody in a dialogue, one of the prime rules is you don't present or advocate for your solution. You stay in the spirit of inquiry. All these forms of conversation, yes we gather, we talk, and what I'm pointing out is that what we aspire to is a conversation that doesn't have a name. That's where we're trying to figure out what's best for everybody. We're being creative and we're being accepting of other people. We're being heartfelt and we're not avoiding our feelings. I didn't give that conversation a name. I call it choice creating as opposed to decision making.

Decision making is where you cut away and use your reason. Choice creating is where you're talking in this creative collaborative way and all of a sudden everybody knows what we're going to do. We don't have to vote. We all know. That kind of conversation is the one we want. Now how do we reliably evoke it and keep it because there are some dangers to that kind of conversation. If you're being creative in that conversation and somebody says no, that's a stupid idea, it hurts to your core. You may never resurface. Once people are in that spirit of choice creating and talking in that spirit, any form of judgment is a killer.

What Dynamic Facilitation does is it is we help people go to that space of talking. It takes a while but we get there. Then we keep people safe. We keep people safe. Then the risk is that once the meeting is over and they go back into their company or into their normal life or whatever, there's all this judgment and this nonappreciation and you feel hurt afterward anyway. The idea really and one of the principles as a Wisdom Council is we keep it going. Is it random selection; they meet, they make a presentation. Is it dialogue; I use the word dialogue, ongoing and then there's another random selection, a different group and we keep this ongoing choice creating conversation alive. This involves everyone.

Nicholas: What's the benefit of a random group as opposed to experts and representatives?

Jim: We have that today, the experts and representatives. We already have our representative group. They gather and they make choices. Then you have experts gathering in the think tanks. The point is that they cannot establish the spirit of choice creating in all of us. If you're a representative, if you're representing some constituency, by definition you're not an authentic person. It's like you're not really in the room.

Nicholas: Because you are taking up a position.

Jim: You take a position and you defend a position and you go to your constituency and find out when you're supposed to say next. It's not an authentic conversation.

Nicholas: A Wisdom Council or the choice creation or Dynamic Facilitation process, you're not saying that that would replace all the current structures but it's something to run in parallel, almost like a board of directors overseeing a charity or something. Like a think tank feeding into an executive body.

Jim: Exactly. It's the conversation that's missing from our current system. That's where we all just stop every so often and say, "How we doing? Do we like what's happening, are we okay with where we're going, is it alright if we're trashing the planet?"

Nicholas: If it's such a great idea, Jim, why hasn't it taken off like wildfire?

Jim: I ask myself that all the time and right now I'm riding Manfred Helrigl's coattails because I've just pulled away because he's the guy who can talk about it and take it forward in a way that isn't threatening. The problem is that when we are authentic like this, we really are vulnerable. Most of us I think are in denial. We are pretending to ourselves that we're honest and we're doing okay. The world is working. It's painful, painful, painful. People think that we're going to help people become aware by telling them. No, if you're in denial, you don't say thank you very much for that information. You just get mad at the people that are telling you stuff.

You get angry and you say get out of here. Go away, I don't want to talk to you anymore. I think that's what is happening is that it's like the drunk knows you should stop drinking but he doesn't want to hear it from anybody, doesn't want to face it. I think once we start this authentic conversation and we really face into what we're doing and where we want to go and what's going on, I think it's just like an earthquake. It's like a traumatic experience in a way. Not at the moment. At the moment, people leave, they're excited, they're pumped.

Every Wisdom Council we've ever done, the people leave pumped, but then you wonder why 2 months, 3 months down the road don't they come to the next one. What's happening here? Why isn't this building, getting traction? I've been asking myself that for a long time and I have decided that it's, like I said, it's so transformational that at one level it's terrible. Once you leave that environment, it just seems really hard to get back to it. That's where it could be maintained.

Nicholas: To me that sounds like you're creating this most amazing group state, an altered state of consciousness and group experience in which people are having, as you say, huge breakthroughs and tapping into the collective wisdom. Then when they go out into the cold, into the rain, and come up against the rest of the world, that's not sustained. That's quite similar to people going on self development workshops or leadership workshops. They have an amazing experience and then they go back to exactly the same situation they were in before with the same instructions, processes, and leadership style and so on. Surprise, surprise, nothing happens.

Jim: Something happens. What happens is that I as a person have exposed myself and been authentic, been present and then we go back into the normal structure and I can feel pain from it. It has to be ongoing in some important way.

Nicholas: Maybe there needs to be alongside it some institutional or structural changes, process changes that actually help the process to embed.

Jim: I think that would be great. I don't know what they are actually. I've always thought about it in terms of the just sneaking it into the system but my book is about, Gee, there should be a Constitutional Amendment in the US. There should be a Constitutional Amendment then we have it ongoing and everybody pays attention and we get it that it's part of the structure of our society that we have this we the people conversation in an ongoing way. I think Iceland is rewriting its constitution and it's a small little country and it's got all these problems so I write to people in Iceland every so often.

I'm trying to slip it in but I must say that the Governor of Vorarlberg which is one of the states of Austria and that committee, the Deputy Governor and both parties are talking about making it a Constitutional Amendment for the State of Vorarlberg because they have so much experience with it in cities.

Nicholas: In a way, companies do this don't they because companies get in, under the heading "marketing," they get in focus groups and so on to get the wisdom of the consumer to better understand the market.

Jim: A focus group is a different thing because the power is in the hands of the people they hire. They set up a focus group to find out what the answer is and then they make their informed decisions. This is not about that. This is about where we the people begin to get it that my goodness, we're in charge and they work for us. Once we become unanimous or unified, this random group meets and they create a unified perspective and the rest of us look in and say, "Yeah, I think so too." That's a lot better than anything else on the table.

Then we look around the virtual room and realize my goodness, all of us think this. Now this is a force. This isn't just a wish. This has an even more than political will. It has the force of hey that's a nice Constitution; let's do this different one. It isn't just operating within the system anymore. We've left the system.

Nicholas: As a process, obviously this would be better suited to particular kinds of people in certain circumstances for certain purposes and there will be other situations to certain types of people in certain challenges or structures and so on where it really wouldn't work at all. If you look across the spectrum of human cultural evolution, at the beginning end that we can see in some of the traditional cultures, some elements still going in parts of Africa in the traditional culture or in the North American Indians or the Aborigines, the process that you're talking about was quite common where the community would have some kind of cultural structure to come together to draw in the different threads to get the wisdom and then the solution would emerge. Then you've got all the stages of development through the empire and the industrial phase and the corporate phase. Then coming out of the other end of that is the pluralistic democracy where it seems to fit quite well as well. It's almost the middle bit where it doesn't seem to fit so well. What's your experience of where the Wisdom Council really works well? Where is it best deployed?

Jim: I think it needs to be everywhere. You're right, it didn't have to be there when you have a system in place that just operates on automatic pilot. We lost track of it. Even there, I think it should be; we should be always in a state of consciousness where we're thinking about whether we want to be in this game that we're playing or maybe some other game or maybe not a game at all. We should be conscious and that's really what this is. This is about bringing here's a way to evoke a collective consciousness.

Because right now we're in a period of collective stupidity. We're trashing the planet. We're destroying our people.

It's just terrifying what's happening and yet most people are still in denial about it. Other people are in denial by assuming certain models of change will happen, like "Be the change you want to see in the world" or have the right perspective or teaching everybody nonviolent communication or communication skills or Dynamic Facilitation or any of those. We can't stay in that small thinking mode. We have to facilitate a collective awareness.

Nicholas: If you look over the Western world since the Second World War, politicians were probably never super popular but they've got less and less popular and really most people, I think probably unfairly, consider them all to be scoundrels and corrupt. Is there any link to that to what you're talking about? Is there a way that politicians, maybe a new generation of politicians, could take the principles you're talking about and run with them successfully?

Jim: I think that the current politicians will do this. I don't think it's bad politicians. I think that the system structures a situation where you have to get money in order to get elected and if you're going to get money, you have to go to a certain set of players and that's just the rules of the game. I think everybody gets elected trying to do what's best. I think that elected officials, if they got it, what this could do for them, they'd jump on it because here's a way they get to be in the conversation I bet they really want to be in about what's best for everybody and then they get to support people to get that and be reelected.

This is a deal where we've never experienced a general interest group before. We just have competing special interests. What this does is it sets in motion the general interest conversation. When the Wisdom Council speaks, they are a legitimate symbol maybe for the first time in history of the general interest, the public interest.

Nicholas: Have you got any experience of doing that with the very hot topics like immigration or what to do about crime or reforming the welfare system, things like that? Create a lot of heat and hot tempers.

Have you applied this process to that sort of thing?

Jim: I've done a lot of that with Dynamic Facilitation just asking for the hot topic because the hot topic helps you in Dynamic Facilitation because it brings more energy. There was a Wisdom Council in Austria where they brought up the issue of where are the immigrants; how come they're not a part of this? We want them to be a part of it, it started out being angry that they were different but then it was like a shift happened and then it was like we want them to be part of it.

I thought it was pretty exciting really because this is in post war Austria where there is a lot of bad feelings about the immigrants and the reality is as soon as people start talking from this heartfelt place, everybody wants them to be involved. They want them to be part of things and then later they did another Wisdom Council and they had some immigrant folk. One guy in particular I remember, I only heard this story, but he had a night shift. He was working on night shift so this was all during the day and then he had to go to his night shift and he couldn't wait to come in the morning and be a part of the next group.

Here he was being accepted and being part of things and so there he was, he hadn't slept in I don't know how many hours. He was a participant in the Wisdom Council and then really excited about it and then I understand that he was very much a leader in the immigrant community of helping people get it that this is what was happening and how to make things happen. I don't know the details but I know that he was a leader. Of course he wasn't until he was randomly selected. Now he's a leader.

Nicholas: People are very critical of politicians but they're not very critical of the media. I think it's true across the world; it's definitely true in the British media that when politicians are interviewed, they're forced to answer questions in soundbites. They're not given an appreciative space. They're not given an hour to speak. They've got to have the answer quickly and it's usually done from a very aggressive point of view. Almost like an aggressive lawyer with the assumption that they're an idiot or they're deceitful or they're partisan and the aim is to trip them up and prove that they're an idiot really.

That doesn't seem a very healthy way. Obviously you've got to be disciplined with them because they can be slippery fish and so on so you've got to be intelligent. What can we ask of the media to improve the quality of our democracy?

Jim: You're going to hear one answer from me the whole time and it's going to be the Wisdom Council fixes everything. Once we start thinking instead of just being on automatic pilot then it changes everything. I believe that the media respond. They're about selling the news. They want as many listeners and they want business and advertisers and whatever like everybody else. They're going to try to find the screw-up right now. That's what they want. They want to find the glitch. They want to find the horrible thing that's going on, the scandal because that's where the attention of the people is. As soon as we start talking, all of us, and figuring out what we really want and the real problems that we have and how to fix them, then it's going to be a different world I think in terms of the media.

Now the media is serving, gets more interest by pointing out the things that are helping us go toward what we all want. It's like during World War II, you'd look at the newspapers from that period and the headlines would be we made little progress in this area and made little progress in that area. That's not what they do today. Nobody pays attention to the progress. If we have that overriding mission that we were a part of, that we all felt connected to like saving the planet, we would be excited in the same way to find this positive news. I think the elected officials would be in the position of serving the public will which is what they want to be doing in the first place.

Nicholas: Maybe this is really obvious to you but I wonder whether it matters who's in charge of this process because in this country, the last Labour government set up a thing which sounded great. It was called the Big Conversation where a road show went around the country with various ministers participating. They generally seemed to want to engage people talking across the whole range of things to tap into the wisdom of the people and access creativity and so on. I'm sure people had great experiences at the time but I never really heard of anything very positive that came out of it constructively.

I wonder whether this process, the Wisdom Council process, is much more powerful if it's something that the population initiates. It's not top down but it's bottom up and therefore people just do it and they might think who are we; we're just a bunch of random people; who cares what we think. I can imagine there's a power in the process that unfolds, that people begin to know it's happening and then listen and then it actually gains in power.

Jim: I think so. My first initial take on it would be it would be a Constitutional Amendment in the US and that's presumably we the people speaking; we the people saying we want this. That's symbolically what a Constitutional Amendment would be. What I discovered is that, boy that's going to be the last step. Getting a Constitutional Amendment in place is like whoa. The exciting discovery was that the amendment isn't essential. It's really about the quality of talking so when the elected officials go and speak in the Big Conversation, they're not having a choice creating conversation. They're having something else in dialogue or probably an interview process. They're in their roles.

You cannot have a choice creating conversation with somebody who's in a role. Yes, I believe that just a group of citizens with resources could set a Wisdom Council process in motion. Really we just need money. That's really what it boils down to. We need money. Now, as an interim strategy, one of the options of the Wisdom Council process, one of the principles is the group chooses the topic. We make compromises all the time and one of the compromises is when the government chooses the topic and we call that a creative insight council as a separate type of Wisdom Council.

One great thing about that is the government gets to do it and they have a budget already. People are interested ahead of time in the topic. They pay attention. It's a way to get things started in a way and really productive thing for government to do.

Nicholas: As far as both your country and my country, their foreign policy for many years has been to export democracy around the world and encourage democratic institutions and so on. What do you think about that? Is that a good thing to do?

Jim: I'm really not so much an expert in the current democracy as I am in the kind that I'm envisioning. I think it's, I don't know if it's good or bad and I think it just comes with the territory. If you set up a system that is a competitive structured system and economy like that and have a debt-based monetary system, it requires growth. It requires economic growth. There's no way around it. It will expand. Do we want that requirement on us? If we thought about it, probably not. We would say maybe we could keep these indigenous languages and maybe we want to think about what we're doing rather than just be on automatic pilot where everybody just has to run and earn more and get more.

You look at anybody in the street outside your building there and you tap them and you realize that that person is trying to sell somebody some more stuff, whatever it is. That's what our system does and requires them to be employed selling more stuff. Even stuff that people don't want but they need to be educated to want. That's the way it works when we export democracy. If we want to think about these, these are choices we're making that we're unconscious about. Collectively we're just doing it. Because of structures that we set up and the way we set up our "democracy," our economics, so forth.

All of us are just carrying on this design that we didn't even think about when we set it up. Now I'm just proposing here's a simple way, an obvious way, an easy way to start thinking and make conscious choices with how we spend our precious resources on this planet, how we spend our human resources, how we work with our children, it's just about thinking.

Nicholas: What you're talking about is a radical culture change or an evolution in culture. How about starting with children and schools. If you can find a way to apply it to that context then they can actually learn the process you're talking about and actually experience it and learn how to make it work and make it effective and then as they grow up, they'll naturally take it to their workplaces and the wider culture.

Jim: I'd certainly never say no to that. I think that's great. I don't think that's going to be tipping the scales. I think the whole idea of the education, being the next generation and the tipping point and the 100th monkey and all that stuff, I think that's a model of change that works really well for nuclear energy and it works for some things but it isn't going to work for this. The reason why it's not going to work for this is because you and I are embedded in a mechanical system. It's like we're on the Titanic and we can educate people this way and that way and this way and that way but there's a certain kind of education we need to have happen and that's for them to notice that we're headed toward an iceberg and that we're on a ship and there's a steering wheel up there. If we just tweak that baby, we can get out of this mess. That's what we need is we need enough of us that are sitting over on the sidelines realizing hey we're on a boat here and we can do the steering. Not the steering, we can facilitate the people to at least steer what we're doing. It isn't us steering. It's us facilitating the people to steer.

Nicholas: I don't know if you've ever been involved in local politics but it can attract some very weird people with bees in their bonnets and particular personalities and of course certain interest groups and so on. I suppose the randomness of the Wisdom Council is meant to filter that sort of thing out.

Jim: Yes, even if you don't get them, it's not that bad. If you hold a town meeting or something, you get the same people. You get the usual suspects and they all have their axe to grind and whatever. You randomly select people. It's random. You get the mainstream people that have been driven away and you want just a pure random selection to show up. You want the left, you want the right, you want the wackos, you want all of it. You're going to engage them in a process of thinking that takes the best, not the worst. We're going to get the highest common denominator, not the lowest.

We're going to put that out there and the point isn't they don't have any power other than when the rest of us hear what they've said, we all go "oh yeah!" that's so much better or even here's something that I think would be better. If you are the one person in the whole country of the UK that disagrees with what the Wisdom Council says, people are going to be interested in; what they heck? Nicholas, talk to us; tell us why would you not go along with this. Now you have a voice. Here you are just one person out there and for some reason, you're thinking differently and we're interested in it. We want to incorporate your views instead of the usual "Holy smoke we got you out voted, you're screwed."

Nicholas: Fantastic. Thank you so much, Jim. I really enjoyed talking to you very much.

Jim: Same here, Nicholas.

Nicholas: Anyone that wants to follow up your work, read your books, or come to one of your trainings or invite you to do this in their town or city, how do they best get in touch with you?

Jim: Either www.dynamicfacilitation.com or www.wisedemocracy.org are good websites too.

Nicholas: Fantastic. Thank you so much.

Jim: Thanks, Nicholas.

Mindfulness

Applications for Leaders and Clinicians

Dr Nicholas Beecroft

"Mindfulness" is becoming a fashionable buzzword. However, there's nothing new about it. It is part of human nature itself. Mindfulness means paying attention, with intention, to the world as it is with an attitude of equanimity. This means that one focuses one's attention upon some of the huge array of sensations arising from within ourselves internally and as a result of our sensing the outside world. Equanimity means the attitude of neither craving pleasant sensations nor having aversion to unpleasant sensations.

To an extent we have to be non-mindful in order to survive. At any time there is a vast amount of information available to us and there's no way which we could possibly attend to it all. However, in Western Civilization we have a tendency to bias our attention towards a mind, ego, thoughts and external objects. We therefore don't make the most of the rest of our body, our heart, gut, intuition, sensing, energetic awareness and so on. In addition, we tend to intentionally anesthetize ourselves with television, junk food, addictions, the Internet, travel, workaholism and so on.

We are all mindful from time to time. Sometimes we are awakened by threats such as illness, accident is, threats to our physical security. We have peak experiences such as great sex, fantastic food and celebrations. Nature often brings us to be more mindful whether it be a sunset, sitting round the campfire, walking along the beach watching the waves or playing whether child. We engineer mindful experiences on purpose such as weddings, funerals and Christmas.

There is now a lot of evidence now that mindfulness brings great benefits. For anyone who practices mindfulness, this evidence comes from the direct experience of the benefits in real life. Other evidence comes from the wisdom passed down through tradition built up over centuries or millennia such as the meditation practice in Buddhism, Tai Chi, Tantra and martial arts. In the last 30 years of so there's been raft of scientific evidence of the effectiveness of mindfulness practice including Mindfulness-Based Stress Reduction which is an 8 week introductory course taught in small groups for one half day a week. This course has been shown to have profound benefits in increasing health, happiness, leadership skills, resilience, freedom, self-discipline, presence, improved eating habits, better self-mastery, reduced relapse of depression and even increased fighting ability of US Marines.

Mindfulness comes in a vast number of forms including meditations such as meditations upon the breath, body scan, heart, anger, gut, eating, sounds and visualizations. Movements can be mindful such as walking meditation, 5 rhythms dancing, martial arts and movement medicine. One can meditate upon compassion, prayer or particular intention. Energetics is mindfulness of energy and higher consciousness. Tantra is mindfulness in the sexual and interpersonal realm. Many people use mindfulness with nature including animals such as equine facilitated learning.

Mindfulness has many clinical applications. For example, to the way in which we respond pain, anxiety, mood changes, external events and cravings have a massive impact on our clinical state. It can make all the difference between being disabled and not disabled and determine one's quality of life.

Below is a transcript of a lecture which I gave entitled "Mindfulness for Leaders and Clinicians" to an audience of clinicians. It includes some practical examples including breathing meditation, heart meditation, eating meditation and awareness of one's interpersonal presence. The purpose of the lecture was to give an introduction to mindfulness to whet the appetite and to encourage people to explore for themselves.

The many links below include a huge range of different types of mindfulness practices which you can explore. Towards the bottom is a list of some of the academic research on the efficacy of mindfulness.

Mindfulness References and Resources
Introduction Self-Help guide (www.get.gg/docs/Mindfulness.pdf)
Simple first stop for a basic overview and summary.

Mindfulness: A practical guide to finding peace in a frantic world
Professor Mark Williams' 8 week course on audio book for the general population

Mindful Leadership & Self-mastery
Three Levels of Power and How to Use Them, Carolyn Myss
Excellent audio book

The Three Levels of Intuition, Carolyn Myss:
Excellent audio book

Presence: Exploring Profound Change in People, Organizations and Society

Synchronicity: The Inner Path of Leadership by Jaworski

The Power of Now: A Guide to Spiritual Enlightenment by Eckhart Tolle

Practising the Power of Now by Eckhart Tolle

Time to Think: Listening to Ignite the Human Mind by Nancy Kline

Vipassana Meditation
Goenke's 10 day courses at Dipa Dhamma

Heart meditation
Open Heart Meditation Free Downloads
Excellent download MP3

The Institute of HeartMath Research Center

The Heartmath Solution: The Institute of Heartmath's Revolutionary Program for Engaging the Power of the Heart's Intelligence by Doc Childre, Howard Martin

Mindful eating
Center for Mindful Eating

MIT Eating Healthfully
Download Hunger scale and Eating Journal

CAMP system for mindful eating

Voice dialogue Technique

Embracing Our Selves: Voice Dialogue Manual by Hal Stone, Sidra Winkelman
Highly recommended way to integrate your inner selves.

Voice Dialogue Articles
By Hal Stone, Ph.D. and Sidra Stone, Ph.D.
See also their videos to describe the technique

Big Mind, Big Heart
Excellent application of Voice Dialogue technique to expand into higher states of consciousness.

Neuroscience of Mindfulness

http://www.youtube.com/watch?v=sf6Q0G1iHBI

The Blissful Brain: Neuroscience and Proof of the Power of Meditation by Shanida Nataraja

Gut Psychology

Gut Instinct: What Your Stomach is Trying to Tell You: 7 easy steps to health and healing by Pierre Pallardy
Excellent practical book

Gut Feelings: Short Cuts to Better Decision Making by Gerd Gigerenzer
Interesting, biased heavily to unconscious cognitions

The Second Brain by Michael D. Gershon
Heavy going but full of scientific detail

Compassion

Compassionate Mind Foundation
Dr Paul Gilbert-check out his excellent book which is both knowledgeable and practical

Enlightenment Intensives
An excellent one of many providers of this intense 3 day Zen/group dynamic training.

Energetics

Soleira Green-New Visionaries & Practical Energetics.
This is a very rich resource indeed. Take a deep look. It's brilliant stuff.

Advanced Energy Anatomy
Carolyn Myss-excellent. I wish it had been taught at my Medical School.

Eastern Body, Western Mind: Psychology and the Chakra System as a Path to the Self by Anodea Judith
Absolutely fascinating book which integrates Western knowledge of anatomy, physiology, neurology, endocrinology with Eastern wisdom about energetics from the Indian Chakra system, Chinese Chi system etc.

The Feminine, The Masculine and Community
Culture of Honouring
Evolutionary-edge project to empower the conscious, masculine and feminine in individuals, couples and community.

Mankind Project
Global organization providing organic leadership training for men.

Equine Facilitated Learning
As Winston Churchill said, "You can learn a lot about the inside of a man from the outside of a horse."

Tantra & Relationships
Great teachers & courses:
Living Love, Jewels Wingfield
Jan Day
Tantra Essence-Mahasatvaa Ma Ananda Sarita

Interesting books:
The Heart of Tantric Sex by Diana Richardson
Tantric Quest: An Encounter with Absolute Love by Daniel Odier

Integrating the body
Movement Medicine
Hard to put into words, great to experience, have a go.

5-Rhythms
Improvised Mindful dancing running through a series of moods

Clinical Applications:
Mindfulness Based Stress Reduction, *University of Massachusetts Medical School*

The Mindful Way Through Depression: Freeing Yourself from Chronic Unhappiness
(includes Guided Meditation Practices CD) by Mark Williams, John Teasdale, Zindel Segal, Jon Kabat-Zinn. Excellent book for relapse prevention in depression and interesting to a much wider audience.

Leading UK Teaching centers of MBCT:
Mindfulness-based Cognitive Therapy
The Oxford Mindfulness Centre
Centre for Mindfulness Research and Practice, Bangor University

Systematic reviews of the scientific evidence

Chiesa A, Serretti A. Mindfulness-based stress reduction for stress management in healthy people: a review and meta-analysis. Journal of Alternative and Complementary Medicine 2009; 15(5): 593-600

Kuyken W, Byford S, Taylor R S, Watkins E, Holden E, White K, Barrett B, Byng R, Evans A, Mullan E, Teasdale J D. Mindfulness-based cognitive therapy to prevent relapse in recurrent depression. Journal of Consulting and Clinical Psychology 2008; 76(6): 966-978

Winbush N Y, Gross C R, Kreitzer M J. The effects of mindfulness-based stress reduction on sleep disturbance: a systematic review. Explore: Journal of Science and Healing 2007; 3(6): 585-591

Grossman P, Niemann L, Schmidt S, Walach H. Mindfulness-based stress reduction and health benefits: a meta-analysis. Journal of Psychosomatic Research 2004; 57(1): 35-43

Baer R A. Mindfulness training as a clinical intervention: a conceptual and empirical review. Clinical Psychology: Science and Practice 2003; 10(2): 125-143

Ospina MB, Bond K, Karkhaneh M, Buscemi N, Dryden DM, Barnes V, Carlson LE, Dusek JA, Shannahoff-Khalsa D. Clinical trials of meditation practices in health care: characteristics and quality. J Altern Complement Med. 2008 Dec;14(10):1199-213.

Wang WC, Zhang AL, Rasmussen B, Lin LW, Dunning T, Kang SW, Park BJ, Lo SK. The effect of Tai Chi on psychosocial well-being: a systematic review of randomized controlled trials. Journal of Acupuncture and Meridian Studies 2009; 2(3): 171-181

Randomized controlled trials
Barnhofer T, Crane C, Hargus E, Amarasinghe M, Winder R, Williams JM. Mindfulness-based cognitive therapy as a treatment for chronic depression: A preliminary study. Behav Res Ther 2009 May;47(5):366-73.

Hepburn SR, Crane C, Barnhofer T, Duggan DS, Fennell MJ, Williams JM. Mindfulness-based cognitive therapy may reduce thought suppression in previously suicidal participants: findings from a preliminary study. Br J Clin Psychol 2009 Jun;48(Pt 2):209-15.

Huffziger S, Kuehner C. Rumination, distraction, and mindful self-focus in depressed patients. Behav Res Ther 2009 Mar;47(3):224-30.

Kitsumban V, Thapinta D, Sirindharo PB, Anders RL. Effect of cognitive mindfulness practice program on depression among elderly thai women. Thai Journal of Nursing Research 2009;13(2):95-108.

Kingston J, Chadwick P, Meron D et al (2007) A pilot randomized control trial investigating the effect of mindfulness practice on pain tolerance, psychological well-being, and physiological activity. J Psychosom Res 62(3): 297–300.

McCracken LM, Gauntlett-Gilbert J & Vowles KE (2007) The role of mindfulness in a contextual cognitive behavioral analysis of chronic pain-related suffering and disability. Pain 131(1-2): 63–9.

Segal, Z., Teasdale, J. & Williams, M. (2002). Mindfulness-Based Cognitive Therapy for Depression. New York, New York: Guilford Press.

Nicholas: My intention is to give a really simple and what I hope is a holistic and practical introduction to mindfulness. First of all, who does mindfulness here? Hands up, who does mindfulness on themselves? Hands up, who does mindfulness with their patients? Fantastic, great, so that's about 10 out of 100 or so.

Well, actually, I think the rest of you didn't answer right because the correct answer is that all of you do mindfulness. Every human who has ever existed and ever will exist does mindfulness. It's just a part human nature just like breathing or eating or standing up in front of people and talking. It's an intrinsic part of who we are. We might not label it as mindfulness but we do it.

What is it? The easiest definition of it is basically two things; one is intentional awareness; intentionally bringing your awareness to whatever the situation of sensations or thoughts, feelings, emotions, events, presence of others, our hearts, our heads, our guts, whatever's going on. So, intentional awareness. The second part of mindfulness is the attitude that we take to that, the way in which we do that. The ideal is curious nonjudgmental, open exploratory attitude so we're available to notice whatever sensations come in. (hearing a loud sound outside the lecture theatre) I just became aware of that sound, I hadn't heard it before. I should have a negative reaction to it and say, "Oh, no, it's going to interfere with my talk. Can people really hear me? I could not even notice it before," but now I'm mindful of it, "I'm aware of the sensations. Don't judge it, don't react, just … isn't that interesting?"

Please, everyone stand up. Choose one other person who's near you and introduce yourself really quickly. Not with words, just body language. You can shake hands if you like. It could just be eye contact. You can just say hello as you normally would and then sit down, thank you. Just put that in your memory bank, we'll do that again at the end. That's just your normal "Hello!"

Second thing, we're just going to do, if you're willing, a couple of minutes of breathing meditation. Make yourself comfortable. You can do it standing, sitting, lying. It's really going to be two minutes. Probably better if you close your eyes. That will reduce my anxiety level but it'll also help you focus your attention. Now, focus your attention on the breath as it comes in and out of your nostrils. Put your intention on the breath coming in and out of your nostrils. Allow yourself to breathe naturally. Notice how you are breathing. You might be doing really small shallow breaths and quite likely bringing your attention to your breath will probably change the way you are breathing but don't assume that. I found as soon as I brought my attention to my breath I suddenly took a big deep breath. Notice the way the air moves as it goes in and out of your nostrils. Notice the change in temperature as it goes in and out.

By the way, remember the attitude-curious, exploratory and nonjudgmental. It's highly likely if you're a human being that at least half of you, your minds will have wondered or found a thought, "I should have gone to the toilet," or, "That noise is annoying me," or, "Who is this guy?" or, "What's for lunch?" That's absolutely fine. When you notice that you simply observe that too with curiosity and gently bring yourself back to your intention to focus on the breath in your nose.

Again, it's highly likely you'll be distracted by the sensations. Maybe you've noticed an itch, a pain, a thought, a memory. Again, if you want to go down that path then follow it. If you would like to bring your attention back to the breath in your nose. Notice the way that your body moves as you breathe. Notice the way that your chest wall moves. Bring your attention to the way that your clothes feel as your chest moves against them.

Then notice your stomach, your abdomen, the skin, the muscle and, if you can, the organs inside. Notice how they move as you breathe in and out. Don't force it, if you get nothing, that's absolutely fine but just curiosity. What sensations do I observe? When I observe a sensation, it could be hot, cold, itch, pain. It might be a nice sensation or a horrible sensation. Just try not to react. Just be open to it. Notice it come. Notice how long it stays and then notice it fade, if it fades.

Then we are going to bring this very brief meditation to a close. You can stay with your awareness of your breath throughout this whole talk, the whole day and then bring yourself back into the room. When you're ready, bring your attention back into the room.

That was a go at being mindful. You probably think, I don't know, you might be thinking, "Well, that's easy, isn't it? We do that. That's ... what's the big deal?" Well, another way to look at mindfulness, what is mindfulness is what is not mindful? If you think about it, well, literally, if you think about it actually. If you imagine a functional MRI scan of your brain, looking at where the blood supply is active in your cerebral cortex, where that little fine bit of attention is focused. We couldn't possibly survive as a being, as an animal if we had to focus on every bit of data coming from our skin, from our heart, making decisions, managing our blood pressure. Are you deciding now whether or not to push the coffee from your stomach down into your small intestine? Of course, you're not. If you were, you wouldn't possibly be able to focus on me. If you were focusing on that, you'd probably fall off your chair because you'd forget your balance. It's completely impossible. We have to choose where we focus our attention to survive.

To a degree, we're naturally unconscious, we have to be. If we were completely unconscious; imagine a boat in a storm. If you've got like a small little sailing boat being hit by waves, being blown by the wind, buffeted around, being knocked around really. Internally, that's like us, with our inner guidance system switched off, we're just reacting as a reflex machine either to sensations that we like and we move towards or sensations that we don't like and we push away. No thinking, but we just act.

The majority of the time that's what we're doing on most things. The practice of mindfulness is to try to just insert a tiny little gap between the awareness of the stimulus, the awareness of the sensation, whether they are physical, thought or emotion or whatever and the reflex action. Just to insert a tiny moment when we have the awareness and hold it and then allow ourselves the freedom to choose how to react.

It may be the freedom to not react, the freedom to let it flow past, the freedom to make a decision and so on. In high-level spiritual terms, the point of mindfulness is to become a super enlightened being. I can't talk much about that because I haven't achieved that state myself. For us more earthbound people, practical people, it's to insert that tiny space to break the chain of our reflexes.

Now, of course, why don't we do that? Why don't we choose to be fully mindful all the time? Partly it's because we wouldn't survive but partly it's also because we don't want to. It's not very nice being aware all the time. If I suddenly focus on my anxiety… I'm not really having any anxiety now I'm pleased to say. If I really wanted to, I could really focus on, "What are they thinking about me? What's that person thinking?" I could actually go down a quite negative path so I'm deliberately going to block that out. I don't want that.

We actually choose to live a lot of our lives with a lot of anesthetics. There's a lot of pain and there's a lot of wounding in ourselves. A lot of you probably don't want to be here. You probably think, "Actually, you know, I'd quite like to go off and play golf," or, "I'd like to go off for a walk," or whatever but you've got to be here. We have to survive in the world. One of the ways we do that is to lock down our feelings and emotions. You could do that mindfully and be aware, "I'm feeling I don't want to be here and I'd rather go home but that's okay, that's a feeling that comes and goes. It passes, I'm not going to react to it or I'm going to react to it."

A common way that we deal with these things actually is to anesthetize ourselves. My favorites are to watch loads and loads of television, drink lots of wine, have lots of comfort food, spend time on the internet, phone a friend and have a meaningless conversation about nothing, go for a walk, go on holiday, be a workaholic. You can spend your whole life deliberately not being mindful. Actually, as medical people you know actually quite often that's when things catch up with you. Just stuff bubbles up underneath the surface it hits us an illness or it hits us as a difficult event.

We all have mindful moments just naturally, not necessarily intentionally. Illness is a good example, an unexpected threat. An awareness of a symptom, walking along the street and you suddenly see a gang. You're scanning, there's a threat. You become aware of your bodily sensations, your presence, your posture. You become aware of your options, your fears. These are negative things that trigger us. There are positive things. We have peak experiences such as an amazing glass of wine, a fantastic sexual experience, an amazing lecture… later in the day, obviously. We actually choose to be mindful. What is a wedding? What is a funeral?

What is the Remembrance ceremony at the Cenotaph in November? It's the point where collectively we decide we are going to choose to bring our attention and our awareness to something.

What are the benefits of mindfulness? There are about three types. The evidence is personal direct experience. You know it's true because you've experienced it. Secondly, randomized controlled trials, studies and meta studies. Then thirdly, wisdom, collective wisdom passed down through traditions in our culture and in other cultures.

What's the evidence? The evidence is that if you're mindful you'll be happier, you'll be healthier, you'll be fitter, less stressed, you have more power, more freedom, more internal mastery, more control over yourself, more choice. Then finally interacting in the world you improve your leadership skills and relationships. If you're mindful, you're going to be bringing your awareness to everything that you do.

Mindfulness is part of human nature and we all do it. A baby could grow up on an island with no human contact it would still work out some form of mindfulness. It would learn to sat on the beach and enjoy the waves or love the food it was eating and so on. Both in our culture and on cultures around the world, people have learnt what works and have refined and distilled practices over many generations. In our culture, because we've industrialized and had a particular way of doing science in our life, we've pushed mindfulness to the edge to some degree but it's much more alive in the traditional Eastern cultures. It's part of the religions like Buddhism, Hinduism, Taoism. It's integral to the way they live and think. There are practices one can do like meditation, Tantric practices, martial arts, Tai Chi, practical things that you can do and learn to do.

If you are anything like me, some people in the audience will be thinking, "Alright, here we go again, mindfulness-another buzzword, another snake oil, another quick fix, another bunch of people with clip boards and, "Come on my course and you'll know everything. You can't do it unless you've been on this course and ticked all these boxes and got the badge" and in 20 years time you'll be recording it on your performance management spreadsheets. Have you done your mandatory meditations today? Yes, tick," and so on.

Yes, I completely have that cynicism myself. It's not about that. Mindfulness is natural, it's in everything that we do. Mindful practices can be meditation. You've done breathing meditation, we'll do a heart meditation, you could do a body scan meditation, you could do an anger meditation, getting in touch with your anger, getting to know it. You can do Tantric meditation, sexual meditations with a partner, looking at all of the energetic experiences between you. You can do energy and spiritual meditations. You could do relating to your job mindfully. You can, as Churchill said, you can learn a lot of about the inside of a man from the outside of a horse. I didn't believe him so I did it-Equine Facilitated Learning. It's amazing what you can experience mindfully learning from a horse. There's a huge variety of options. You can do martial arts mindfully, you can walk mindfully, you can also eat mindfully.

Let's take an example, heart mediation. This is one that I'd like us to have a go at. Now, in Medical School it's taught that the heart is a pump. It obviously is. It also regulates our blood pressure, fluid balance and so on. I remember learning all the cardiac neuroanatomy. The idea was pretty much that there's break and a pedal, faster and slower and there wasn't much notion of anything going back to the brain. Of course, in our cultural wisdom we know that there's more to it than that. We all say this person is Temperamentally Unsuited to military service because their heart's not in it anymore. They are not passionate, they don't care. Or when you're making a decision, "Shall I buy this house or not?" You can go round and round and round and round and round and loops neurotically ruminating, unable to decide and then you can say, "Alright, hold on, what does my heart say? What does my gut say? What does my spirit say?"

Now, there's a group of people in America called the HeartMath Institute. For about 20 or 30 years they've been doing studies into the heart from the perspective of meditation, awareness, the connection between the heart and the brain in decision-making, in judgments, in love, in connection and specifically also for this audience, how it relates to anger, how it relates to anxiety and so on and health. (Look below at the links you'll see there's a massive evidence.) Heart meditation is great for blood pressure, it's great for reducing the risk of relapse with heart attacks. Bizarrely people who have a pet dog are 50 percent less likely to have a second heart attack. It's believed that's because of a connection with the heart because dogs are very heart centered and open the heart.

They've done studies in organizational settings, into businesses and got people to practice heart meditation regularly. There's a reduction in anger, reduction in conflict and increase in cooperative behavior, a decrease in absenteeism, better connection with vision. Quite a lot of people leave because they say, "I never wanted to be here, I'm off." Other people really tap into their passion and their productivity increases. The only thing unfortunately they haven't yet shown is that it increased profits. Of course, as soon as they do that then it will really take off. It's amazing evidence so do look it up.

I'm going to show you a heart meditation. If you want to do it later you can download it from links below. Make yourself comfortable. Bring your awareness to your body. Take a nice breath. Really open up your chest. Really take some nice deep breaths right down into your abdomen. Feel your bum on the chair, your feet on the ground and if you would like to, I would suggest you close your eyes to increase your focus on your heart.

Now I would say before doing this, this isn't a dangerous thing to do because you are what you are. When we do this, you might get a really loving, beautiful, transcendent love experience but also you might get some pain come up. If you've had a bereavement or if there's some pain in your heart you might experience that. If you're worried about that don't do it, don't do it now if you're not comfortable with that. Nothing dangerous can happen but it can unlock stuff. Make your own judgment as to whether you want do that.

Now, those of you who are left, which I hope is everybody, just take your fingers and place them over the center of your chest. Just in the center over the sternum. The point of that is, like an American President singing their national anthem, is to remind yourself to focus your attention there in your heart.

Now I want you to put your attention underneath your fingers on the skin underneath the center of your chest and then bring your awareness, your attention to the skin underneath your fingers. Do this with curiosity, open-mindedness and non-judgment. It's an experiment, it's playful, it's light, there's no right answer, if nothing happens that's fine, no big deal. Just go with it. If you want to stop at any time, please do.

Allow your attention to go a little bit underneath, a couple of inches deep under. I know biologically your heart's off to the left but energetically, spiritually, neurologically, sensation wise, it's more in the center functionally. Just allow your attention to go a little bit under the skin. Now keep your attention there with openness, curiosity, noting whatever sensations. Any warmth, any cold, any twitches, any itches, any pain, any tightening, any tingling, absolute … and nothing, if there's nothing that's great too. Don't react, there's no right answer, it's just interesting.

Now bring to your mind someone or something that you absolutely love. It could be a loved one, it could be your pet dog, your pet bunny rabbit, it might be someone from memory or if you don't have anyone like that it could be someone from fantasy or imagination or it might just be a really beautiful experience you've had, like a really peak experience that was wonderful. Bring that to your mind. As you do that, bring your attention and awareness to what's happening underneath your hands, underneath the skin. I'm going to shut up briefly, just allow whatever is there to be there.

(20 seconds pause.)

This is a bit like lighting a fire. Those of you where the fire is already lit and you've got some sensation there, let go of the images and focus upon the sensation and let that fire burn bright. I'm not seeing many smiles in the room so I'll say it again. Bring to your mind someone or something that you love and observe the sensations underneath your hand in your center of your chest, in your heart. If you find yourself smiling just smile back at the heart and the sensation and stoke up the fire. Let that get stronger and stronger and keep breathing and smile back at your heart and really enjoy that feeling. By the way, if it's a negative feeling, if it's a bereavement, if it's a pain, if it's a loss, if it's a hatred, just accept, open and embrace that too. Just observe it, it is what it is.

Those of you where that's taken, stop listening to me for a while and keep focussing on the sensation in your heart. I'll speak to those where it hasn't taken off and we'll go again with patience, bring your attention back to the center of your chest, bring to mind someone or something that you really love and observe whatever sensations come. Hot, cold, warmth, gushing, intense anger, deep sadness, whatever it is. If you find yourself smiling, smile back and soak it up and get it going. Basically, keep going through that loop. Now I'm going to be quiet for a minute and let us all do that together. If you want to stop then stop.

(60 seconds pause.)

Keep breathing. If you've got something going there like a fire, imagine you can breathe in and out of your heart directly. Breathe in and out and let it expand and grow and let the feeling expand throughout your body and maybe expand vastly beyond your body. Whatever is happening to you is just the right thing.

(20 seconds pause.)

Now over the next 30 seconds or so allow your protector-controller self to gently rein that in, whether that's a beautiful experience or a painful one or just an interesting one or nothing and bring your attention safely and gently back to the whole you. Stay in connection with that if you choose but bring it to your whole body, presence of others around you. Remember to leave a safe boundary around yourself, appropriate, protective boundary then bring your awareness to the whole room and to me.

You'll have had a whole range of experiences there. Some people went to like a Tantric bliss state. Some people looked out the window and really didn't want to do it, fine. Some people had some pain, some people were curious; some people were trying but not getting much. Some people had a chat with the person next to them. Whatever happened is absolutely fine. Some people can do that just like that, at the first attempt. The first 20 times I tried that I got nothing. It's like everything, if you practice you can get better and better and better, access it really quickly. If you can access that in easy times then in difficult times, when you're having an argument, when you're trying to discipline somebody, when you've got a decision to make, when you're giving a lecture. You can access the wisdom of your heart and the heart-brain connection.

What has this all got to do with clinical work? Look below to look at the research if you want all the facts and figures. In a practical way, what's the use of this, you know sitting with a patient. If you take for example a pain. We all get pain but definitely we have patients who have pain. Some pains come and go and they are transient, we don't even think about them. Others are overwhelming and catastrophic, and terrifying and so on.

One of the things that you'll all be aware of is that you can get two patients or two selves who have exactly the same apparent physical pathology, the same cancer, the same physical trauma, the same punch in the face, whatever it is. If you looked at it through an electron microscope, the physical thing, it is the same but people react enormously differently. You can get one person who reacts to that pain with a cascade of fear, a cascade of catastrophic thoughts and then a whole load of reactions, shutting down the world, shutting down their life, withdrawing into fear, stopping their job, not having sex, not going into work, "My life's over," etcetera, etcetera, going into depression, going into hopelessness. You can have another person for whom the same illness is like water off a duck's back. They didn't dissociate from it, there's no big deal. You can get someone else who really is in pain and can sit with the pain. It's not nice, they'd rather it wasn't there but they kind of say, "Yes, there it goes again. It's not very nice. I'm not going to react to it. I know there are a few strategies I can use to reduce it but it's going to go away."

Mindfulness practices are basically ways of practicing that skill and to get better at it. If you're going to practice it at the most difficult time when you really need it, that's not really realistic.

Now obviously that principle applies to everything. It applies to anxiety, when an anxious feeling, an anxious thought, an anxious mood comes or in relationships, someone said something, someone does something, something happens. If we can just get that tiny slither of a gap in between the sensation arising and the reaction then we a have a choice, we have a freedom and we have a bit more chance to do something differently.

In the remaining time, I will say a bit about the scientific evidence, we're going to do an eating meditation and then we're going to do the handshake again in a super mindful way with mega presence.

What's the evidence for it? To a degree, the evidence is three types. One is your own evidence. If you do it, if you practice it, if you experience it, it's completely obvious and you don't need to read about a randomised controlled trial, end of story. If you're talking about deeper practice like meditation, like Tai Chi, like Tantra, like meditation in nature, like practices that cope with pain, that's kind of handed down through wisdom, through experience, through generations of people who've tried it, who've perfected the techniques, who know how they work and who can tell you about it. They have the wisdom and experience level.

I'm a total believer in science by the way, but what we narrowly call science, the objectifying falsifiable, reductionist science; amazingly, that's even been done for mindfulness. One of the leaders in that is a guy called Jon Kabat Zinn. There are many but he is one of the pioneers. He is someone who's stripped away the baggage from the East and kind of stripped away the cultural baggage, the religious baggage, the spiritual baggage and just reduced them to practical psychological how to do this tools, mixed it with our Western psychological individual and group techniques and tested them out and practiced them.

They've produced a course, a standardized package which is tested, it's brilliant. It's called Mindfulness-Based Stress Reduction. It comes in other forms. People have applied it for Cognitive therapy for depression, they call it Mindfulness-Based Cognitive Therapy. Later we will do some Mindfulness-based eating which is for people with eating issues.

The core package is the same. There's an eight-week course, it's about half a day and it involves eight to 10 people learning the breathing meditation, they do a body scan meditation, they do a yoga meditation, they do an awareness of attitude and body. They do awareness of sounds. Then they practice things like mindful walking and mindful eating. Each person keeps a diary of how they have tried to stuff out what they've done and they bring it back to discussion to ground it.

You all know from eight-week courses that are half a day a week, you've probably been on loads that were interesting that could change your life. Some people will be transformed but most will just have an interesting experience. The amazing thing is there've been loads of follow up studies in lots of different contexts and I mean lots. Hospital inpatients, physical rehabilitation, pain units, anxiety patients, eating disorder patients, people with all these conditions we are not very good at treating like fibromyalgia, back pain, things like that.

Across the board, there's massive improvements in the experience of symptoms, in the quality of life and in some cases in getting better, improved blood pressure. It really does sound like snake oil, you know these magic potions from the Nineteenth Century. "Take this and it makes everything better," but there is something about mindfulness practice which really does bring us into our natural healing and our natural physical state, our groundedness, which is good for us, simple as that.

Now the quality of the research is so good that the most hard people on earth, other than the Syrian secret police, the American HMOs, the Health and Management Organizations, the American health insurance companies. If you know anything about them, they will pay for nothing that doesn't work. They pay for these mindfulness courses in inpatients across all kinds of conditions. Even orthopedic surgeons who you'd have thought would be the last to try out these sorts of things. It get patients better faster, they leave faster, they heal quicker and they come back less sick.

A specific example is eating behavior. You can tell I'm not super slim so you might say, "He's going to tell me about eating behavior?" Well, imagine how fat I'd be if I hadn't tried some mindful eating. The mindfulness-based stress reduction approach has been applied to people with bulimia and with comfort eating. It's just an example and it's only really been getting going for the last five years. The research is just really unfolding but amazing results so far. Anyone that knows anything about eating disorders and comfort eating; it's really difficult to treat. There's a massive multibillion pounds industry on diet and eating. If anyone had the quick answer for this, it would have come up by now.

There's huge benefits from this. Lots of people are finding after this eight-week course, not just after a week but after follow up periods like

12 weeks, six months ahead that people with long standing difficulties, not the most extreme cases but relatively average people and people with bulimia are getting more control over their eating, more sense of power, more sense of choice, they're enjoying their food more, they're losing some weight so it's looking good.

Part of that is how to eat mindfully. Can I have, say, four volunteers to pass these strawberries around the room? Take 2 each. We're going to mindfully eat some strawberries. By the way, you don't have to like strawberries, I don't like strawberries. I chose strawberries because they are interesting. So long as you're not allergic to it; it's irrelevant whether you like it. Fantastic, now please … oh, I should have said, who's eaten one already while we're waiting? Who's eaten one? (Several culprits confess.) That's okay. Did you do it mindfully?

Strawberry eater: No!

Nicholas: Well, you can tell by look of me there's an awful lot of Chinese takeaways I've shoveled down in front of the television and only noticed it on the last mouthful. If you're anything like me you might experience this as torture because we are going to take ages to eat this strawberry so please bear with me. Actually, you'd lose a lot of weight if you ate everything like this.

If anyone is allergic to strawberries don't eat it. Don't eat it, don't touch anyone! First of all just look at the strawberry. Hold it in your hands and have a look. First of all, just think, where has this come from? I bought it here, it came in my car from London, I washed it in my sink this morning. I bought it in Petersfield yesterday, in Marks & Spencer's, so it's a nice one, not an Asda one. (laughter) Can you tell the difference, taste the difference or smell the difference?

Who knows how it got there? It came in a large truck, it came from some depot. A man … presumably a man, drove it there. Someone somewhere would have picked it. It's British by the way. Where do they come from? Yes, it's a British one, the farm is written on the packet. I didn't mindfully read it, I don't know where. Where is it from Stewart?

Stewart: Kent.

Nicholas: Kent, I'm from Kent, there's the Kent strawberry, someone will have picked it. Quite likely, they were an overseas temporary Polish or Portuguese worker who comes across in the summer. My granddad used to do that as a boy down from Brixton where he used to live, they used to pick them so I'm feeling a family link. I used to live in Kent and, as a boy, we used to go into the fields and pick these. Quite often, we wouldn't pay for them. Sometimes, we would.

Now think about, how did this come about? This thing is covered in seeds. Why are we even holding it? What does it mean in terms of nutrition for you? Why does the plant put these seeds on it that make it tasty so that we and other animals would want to eat it? What's the point of that? How many of these seeds pass through us? We won't be too mindful about what happens after that but if you imagine at some point some animal in a river might eat it and then deposit it on the riverbank with some fertilizer and then we might have strawberries down by the river. You can take that to the nth degree.

Hold this in your hands and think this is made up of atoms but actually, it's not, they don't really exist, it's just a bunch of energy in wave forms. That's weird, isn't it? It's got a mass. Who's experiencing the mass that you're holding in your hand? Now look at the color, look at that beautiful green, that really lush green and look at it really closely to really enjoy it. What a gorgeous color. Look at the way that it's not just one green, there's 100 different greens there. Look at each of those leaves. Look at the hairs, look at the edges, look at the bits that have been nibbled off. Who did that?

Now look at that really gorgeous red color. Well you might hate it, I'm saying gorgeous, I said gorgeous. (Laughs) We've got some gobblers at the back. Make sure you've got an extra in a moment. Now look at that beautiful red color. Again, it's not just one red, how many different reds can you see? Actually, if you look closely, it's not just red, the seeds are … is that green, is it yellow, is it brown, some are black? You might even have a little insect on yours. It might have jumped on to you; it might currently be feeding on you.

Okay, obviously you can do that for another 10 years so ... don't eat it yet. Have a smell, really take a smell. Notice the smell. (A lady in the audience recoils from her neighbors strawberry, laughing) Oh, sorry, are you alright? (Laughs) So we've got someone who really hates the smell of strawberries. She's observing, her gastric sensations, her breakfast is contemplating a return visit due to that smell. What does that do to you? Our smell is our most primitive and one of our strongest senses going straight into the olfactory system in the frontal lobe of the brain. What is that doing to you? What memory is coming up? When have you had a strawberry before? You might hate this, you might want to be sick, you might love it. It might be reminding you of Wimbledon; it might be reminding you of a romantic dinner you had.

Finally, before we go to the next stage, we're going to do this annoyingly slowly (laughter). We're going to go through different bits of this to work out how much we want this strawberry or don't want it. First of all, with your eyes, put your attention on your eyes and look at the strawberry. With your eyes, put your attention on your eyes and your relationship between your eyes and the strawberry. How much do your eyes want to eat this? Score if for yourself out of ten. Mine's about a four.

Now come down to your mouth. Bring your awareness to your tongue, your salivary glands, the insides of your mouth and invite your mouth and your tongue, how much do they want to take this into your mouth? What's the score out of ten? Is it a lot? Is it zero? Is it ... whatever.

Now go back to where we were with the heart meditation. Bring your attention to your heart, center of your chest, go inside, think of someone or something you love. Now invite your heart, open your heart to the strawberry, I bet you've never heard that said before. How much does your heart want to invite the strawberry into your body? Ask your heart intelligence. Mine is higher actually than my mouth. It's about six.

Now everyone swallow and imagine there's like a fist shaped thing going down your esophagus into your gut. Imagine that your brain is now down here and invite your gut. Go into your gut, your second brain. Your gut has got a brain as big as a cat's brain, though not always as lovable. Ask your gut, how hungry are you? There might be hunger, or there might be a gut instinct; yes or no, decision-making gut or it might be both. How much does your gut want this strawberry?

Now go into your being. That's the one who's been doing all this stuff. Not the ego thought one but the one who's observing, the one who's been watching, the one who's behind, the one who's listening. I don't know how you experiencing your being. It might be a little bit here, (head) it might be here (heart), it might be this shape (an egg around the body), it might be as big as a universe. Go into your being one, your energy being and ask your whole being, this sounds weird, doesn't it but how much does your whole being want to take in this strawberry?

Okay, you've found out how much you want to eat it. Now finally the last tantalizing bit. Your lips are amongst the most sensitive parts of your body, corresponding to a large part of the parietal sensory cortex. Run the strawberry over your lips. Feel the temperature, feel the way it feels on your lips, feel the texture, the hairs, the coolness. Again, inviting your body, how much do I want to push this a bit further? Or I have already pushed it further? At long last, if you want to gently take the first nibble and do it really slowly, really mindfully. Don't gobble it down! Chew slowly and hold it in your mouth enjoying or not enjoying, experiencing the flavors, the smell, the taste.

As you do, invite all those parts of you, the mouth, the heart, the gut, your being itself to really share this experience. I don't really like strawberries that much but this one tastes really good. Enjoy it, notice the tip of the tongue. It's like a wine tasting, the front of the tongue, the middle of the tongue, the back of the tongue, side of the mouth. As you swallow it notice the throat, what's the after taste? How does it feel as it slips down? Does it get stuck or does it go all the way down?

How is your tummy feeling about receiving this? Does it want more? Does it like it? Do you feel calmer? Do you feel happier? Do you feel tense? Do you want to spit it out? Just enjoy it. Be aware of it, mouth, heart, gut, being. You can eat the green bit if you like.

Finally, I'd like you to stand up and pair with the person that you said hello to earlier. Now, if you don't mind, be quiet, so no talking, just nonverbal. No talking, no sounds, just nonverbal. First of all, make sure you have a healthy safe boundary; we don't want anyone getting too Tantric. You can do that later if you want to but just for this, a safe healthy appropriate boundary, have that in place. I'd like you to invite you simply connect with the other person bringing your full presence, and if you would choose to I would say, as much as you're willing to. Your full presence so look at them.

Now bring your attention back, no talking, bring your attention into your body, into your heart. Take a breath into your heart and now back out and observe them, feel them. Be aware of their heart or not as the case may be. Nice deep breath, be aware of your gut and their gut. By the way, if you really don't want to look at them, that's fine, that's mindfulness too. You might want to kiss them, hug them, you might hate them, you might find it embarrassing, it's all mindfulness. Whatever it is, it's true.

Lastly, imagine you are the most amazing, most presence-full person like the Queen or the Dalai Lama. Bring your full presence to this person, to this moment. Make them feel like this is the most magical important meeting they've ever had. Bring yourself fully and authentically to this meeting. You can shake hands if you like, you can hold hands, you can do whatever you like. You can just stand and look into their eyes or you can do a quiet nod and say goodbye. Thank the other person for this connection. (Applause)

Evolutionary Leadership

Conscious Leadership in an Age of Transition

Peter Merry interviewed by Dr Nicholas Beecroft

Peter Merry is an evolutionary leader who operates at the evolutionary edge of our civilization. He describes himself as a the human being, author, speaker, global activist, leader, consultant, trainer, synnervator, human ecologist, father, folk singer, theatre director, rugby trainer, husband and energy worker. He spent many years facilitating a leading change in a variety of organizations including traditional corporates and leading-edge transnational organizations. He has been pioneering the practical application of energetics and wisdom including the new technique of systemic energy tuning. In this interview Peter says that his big picture vision for the state that were in, the painful death of an old civilization, and the parallel emergence of a new one. He believes that we are best off if we put our energy fully into the creation and experimental emergence of this new civilization. There is no guarantee of a positive outcome but there are enough signs of evolutionary change to be optimistic.

At the leading edge, people are beginning to understand that we are truly connected as one whole living system which includes the Earth itself. Peter says that by making this perceptual shift we more easily understand the feedback which the Earth is giving us through, for example, climate change so as to enable us to live more in tune with life itself.

He believes that there is going to be a rebalancing of consciousness towards a more natural order with healthy, conscious expressions of masculinity and femininity, healthy hierarchies, healthy boundaries within an increasingly self-organizing living system. By this, he does not mean a reactionary, traditionalist revival but rather a deeper tuning in to a true nature, fully lined with the underlying natural order. A more enlightened approach to science which integrates wisdom, intuition and complexity is going to be essential in that endeavor. Peter describes how we can integrate the shadow, dark parts of our consciousness as individuals and as a whole in order to liberate our full potential.

Peter describes how he uses technique of systemic energy tuning to work with organizations to maximize the potential through aligning closely with life force and nature. He discusses how that might be applied to harness capitalism for good. Our world has become so complex that to take a mechanical, problem-solving, reductionist approach becomes ever more complex and difficult. He believes that, amongst others, this technique is part of the simplicity on the other side of complexity.

Peter gives his view on the healthy integration of the fast-growing Islamic population in the Netherlands. He does not agree with the ethnocentric solutions offered by Geert Wilders and other "right wing" politicians. However he believes that they provide a useful service in bringing the attention of the previously complacent postmodern political elite to the need for Holland to have a healthy identity, strong structures and conscious, world-centric strategies to make a success out of immigration whilst defending democracy, freedom and pluralism. He is optimistic that the Netherlands will provide a positive role model for other countries in this respect.

Peter is Executive Vice-President of Ubiquity University Undergraduate Programs, the founder of the Center for Human Emergence, Netherlands, formed in 2005 to facilitate the Netherlands through the current transition and learn for the world, and a Synnervator in CHE Synnervate. He is Director of Wisdom University in Europe; the founder and Director of the Hague Center for Global Governance, Innovation and Emergence, founded in 2008 to support, learn about and promote innovative integral approaches to the global challenges that humanity faces today; a partner at Engage!, a Fellow of the Center for Human Ecology in the UK where he did his MSc with a thesis on the future of work and economics; As well as working on a PhD at Wisdom University, he is completing his final year (2012) of vocational training in ECOtherapy.

His books are: Evolutionary Leadership, The Pain and the Promise, Leading from the Field

Visit www.petermerry.org

Nicholas: Peter Merry, welcome to the series "Exploring the Future of Western Civilization."

Peter: Thank you. Pleasure to be here.

Nicholas: For those that don't know Peter, I found it quite hard wondering how to introduce him because the conventional phrases would not really capture who he is. For me, I'd describe him as someone who genuinely is an evolutionary leader of the evolutionary edge of our culture, someone who has done a lot of work facilitating change in organizations, both traditional ones, corporate ones and new emerging transitional organizations.

He's founder of the Center for Human Emergence in the Netherlands, which is part of a global network of integral and spiral dynamic facilitators, thinkers and actors, a meshwork. He's Chief Innovation Officer at Ubiquity University and director of Ubiquity's Wisdom School in Europe. He's founder and director of the Hague Center for Global Governance, Innovation and Emergence. He's partner at Engage which is all about earning a living by doing what we're passionate about. I should say, actually, that he's in the Netherlands but where I am in the UK, he's fellow of the Centre for Human Ecology. He's currently working on his PhD at the Wisdom School and recently completed his final year of vocational training in ECOtherapy which I think you call something else in English. What do you call it?

Peter: I refer to it as systemic energy tuning.

Nicholas: I think you've written one book and there are two in the pipeline. He's written a great book which I really recommend called Evolutionary Leadership and there are two on their way, The Pain and the Promise and Leading from the Field. Peter, does that capture the story?

Peter: Yes. (laughs)

Nicholas: Reasonably.

Peter: That's right.

Nicholas: He's also a father ...

Peter: I live in this ecological town in the Netherlands. I'm a father of three little boys and that's all a big part of the story. I sing in a folk band and that all belongs ... Yes.

Nicholas: Fantastic. If I could kick off with the big picture question, what is the state of Western Civilization?

Peter: What's the state of it? I think we could say without a doubt that it's in transition but I think it's in a certain kind of transition which is nonlinear in its nature. I think what we're seeing is the form and the belief systems and paradigm, which shaped Western Civilization falling apart in many different ways. People finding that the current way of thinking about the world is proving inadequate to the reality they're experiencing, finding that the way they organize themselves, the way they've been trained to lead is proving inadequate to the complexity and intensity of change. We're in what Lazlo would call a chaos point, really where the old system is falling apart and the new one hasn't crystallized enough yet for it to be able to take over the helm so people haven't really got a handle on things at the moment, so I'd say we're in that phase right now.

Nicholas: There have always been doom mongers and people who've said, "Everything's coming to an end." How did you know things are really that challenging rather than just we're experiencing life as normal?

Peter: Just look around at the multitude of issues that are coming to a head. Apart from anything else, the way the climate is just this year, I think it's not something that's coming. I think it's here. Just all the weather records that have being broken this year. Just take the last few weeks and the massive drought that's been in the US and then people are linking it up and saying, "Look how that's going to affect world food prices. Now look how the world food prices are going to affect social instability. Look how social instability is going to provide feeding ground for extremism. Look how that's going to feed into global pandemics." The whole thing is interlocked. A single issue is multiple issues that are converging and feeding into each other.

I think even if we take the climate issue, you're seeing all these feedback loops reinforcing each other as in Siberia, the permafrost starts to melt then the methane is released which increases the instability of the climate so the whole thing is reinforcing itself. That's why I think it's an intensity of change which we've not seen for a while. Probably epochal, new era coming.

Nicholas: When you say we're going into a new era or a transition, do you think it's predetermined? Is it clear what's going to happen or is it all up in the air and with many possible futures?

Peter: It's both, in a way. It seems to me like there's a general pattern unfolding of some of the qualities that if it is to take form, this new civilization will have, so that's beginning to shape up and at the same time what that's going to look like in terms of how we organize ourselves in our societies, in our governance, in or organizations, our communities, how all that's going to look like in terms of our own behavior. All of that's still up in the air and the question of how much of humanity is going to be there at the end of the transition to give form to that civilization is also up in the air.

I don't think, I don't believe anyway that it's up in the air, whether humanity as a species or Homo sapiens as a species will make it through. I think we're going to make it through. Quite how many make it through is up in the air. I think we're going to make it, through.

Nicholas: Do you have your own particular vision? Do you see an exciting positive way forward?

Peter: I see a positive outcome and the way forward is certainly going to be exciting. I think what happens in these moments is two things happen at the same time. There's increasing breakdown and stress and pain and suffering and there's increasing breakthrough, innovation, discovery and in the end, the positive energy that comes with that. I think they're going to intensify exponentially at the same time as we move forward. What's important is what you put your attention on.

If we hold onto the old and put our attention on what's falling, then it'll pull us with it. If we put our attention on what's emerging, then that's what we align with and that's what will start to manifest and attract what's in our own lives as well. I do think there's a role to play in the old and that's really a hospicing role. How do we help the old systems to die gracefully so they can fertilize the soil for the new rather than toxify it in a painful struggle of really trying to hold on when actually it's wanting to let go?

In fact, the other day, I got an insight, coming out of a deep meditation practice that actually the old system is one that is already dead. What's happening is that we are keeping it in the twilight zone, by trying to hold onto it. Actually, what it's wanting to do is to be given a ritual burial and honored for the contribution it's made but then ritually closed so it can pass, as it were, into history, into the other domains.

It's haunting us like a ghost at the moment because we're still giving it lots of attention and then particularly when we start to fight against it, we actually turn it into zombies that suck and draw energy. It's like, "Oh, maybe it's already dead and it's dead but not buried. It needs to be dead and buried with ritual and honor."

Nicholas: Yes, that's interesting. It reminds me of a conversation I had with Bishop Michael Nazir-Ali who said, through a Christian lens, that we're living on past spiritual capital. It's there but it's in decay. What is emerging then, what should we be putting our attention on?

Peter: I think there are two different perspectives to look at it from. One is the one which is more common currency, which is making sure that in the way that we evaluate our activities that we include impact on planet, impacts on people, the more classic sustainability story which is basically upgrade of the current paradigm that says if we're going to use money as an exchange system, use our current accounting as the model to work by, then let's make sure that we internalize the true costs of what we're doing so that the price we pay for things and the way we make decisions is an accurate reflection of the value of stuff in the world.

That, I think may be more of a stepping stone than actually, the place we're going because what's going on is actually a nonlinear phase in evolution. The previous civilizational leaps have been nonlinear which means you can't actually see what that's going to look like from the old lens, so upgrade of the current system is not going to be an accurate picture of how it's actually going to look. It's like if somebody gets the image while they go walking into a cave hundreds of years ago where we're monks transcribing a bible or something and trying to explain the internet and that kind of a difference but whereas maybe two years ago, I was saying, "We don't have any signs of what's emerging. We just have to focus on the process of enabling emergence, create the conditions, being and not knowing, being and be curious, help old stuff fall away."

I think we are beginning to see indications of some of the qualities of what's beyond the current paradigm. It's to be found I think where you see the new science and the ancient wisdom traditions beginning to meet in a sense of a reconnection between mind and matter. It's going to be an increasing realization that actually everything that we see and experience around us is composed of energy which quantum physicists have been saying since 1970 and spiritual traditions from how many thousands of years. Anything, even these physical things around us, you look at them under a microscope, they're all moving. They look solid but they're all just energy.

A thought that we have is energy as is an emotion we have. It's like what they showed at Princeton University, 28 years of research in the engineering department, that without statistical doubt, human intention affects the otherwise random nature of events. When a computer generates zeros and ones randomly, even if you have someone on the other side of the world trying to get more zeros or ones on the computer, it has a statistical impact.

It's all proven without a doubt. The question is how does that perspective begin to trickle down into the collective consciousness because it doesn't fit our Newtonian paradigm, the way we've been trained to think about the world. It's going to involve an understanding but also a felt sense of deep interconnectedness of everything.

Now, as we begin to look at and get an understanding of say some of the universal geometric principles for example, understanding the implication of some of Buckminster Fuller's works or some of the stuff that Nassim Haramein has been discovering about the science of the vacuum. We're beginning to start to be able to put language on the process that connects up a unified field and the material reality, what it actually looks like, what the design principles are of light at that level of the whole creation process, the torus being one of the key forms, it seems, to be emerging around that and the physics of the torus.

Nicholas: What is the torus?

Peter: Torus is like, if you look at a weather system that swirls like a vortex but then it comes in and out at both ends and cycles round and around. NASA has some great images of galaxies. They look like this, they have this bulb at the top and they have a bulb at the bottom. The energy is doing this and it's manifesting out here but there's a dynamic between two poles, one which is a more energetic, let's say, subtle pole and the other which one is more gravitational. There's a combination of expansive light in a way and gravitational pull into matter that somehow then creates the manifest reality at the center. In that way that combination of Heaven and Earth or force and intention and manifestation.

I think what we're beginning to discover or rediscover or discover anew or whatever is that there's a whole world of life that exists beyond the physical world that we can see and whatever language we chose to use to describe it or give names to it, that that dimension of reality has a role to play in the manifestation of coherent reality. Once we start to realize that we don't have to work it all our ourselves but there's actually a whole domain of beings or life forms or energies that exist outside of our normal perception and they have a role to play, then the whole thing becomes far less effort. We start to co-create with another dimensions of life that we've forgotten about and never come across before.

Nicholas: Peter, you've been doing some fascinating work for many years in lots of contexts. I'd like to run across a few practical contexts to see how you see things emerging. What about in the family, the relationship between the masculine and the feminine, between the adult and the child. How does this all relate to that context?

Peter: Speculation really, but if I lean into that, I think one of the things that's happened as we reach this end phase of our civilization is there's been a blurring of identities where the feminine has felt it needs to adopt, take on some of the masculine. The masculine itself has needed to take on some of the feminine. I think that's been an important process of each of those two being able to become familiar with the other, being able to respect it and a feel for it.

My sense is what's going to come next is more of a return of the natural order but from an informed perspective where the masculine and feminine do what they naturally do. It's an understanding of how co-creation works as each of those energies steps into its true power, its true place in the system which doesn't mean all this form that we would associate with it traditionally, like the women needs to stay at home with the kids or whatever. The masculine goes out to hunt and kill and bring back the money. Not at all but there is something about sense of a return of natural order where we've blurred those lines in our efforts to integrate everything and everything's equal and the same. I see that coming back.

Also in parenting actually as well. I feel the kids haven't been given the natural boundaries that they might need in their evolutionary process. If we understand the natural evolution of the individual, we see there are moments where the thing children need most are boundary, rules, agreements, structure. In our postmodern thinking, trying to see them as an equal with equal value as a human being but they're not quite the same in terms of where they are in their development. When we try to treat them as equals and involve them as an equal decision making player and don't take our responsibility as parents to draw boundaries and take decisions then they struggle because they're not given the pathway of natural development that we ourselves have been given to get to where we are. So that's again about natural order.

There is a certain place we have and children have need of that natural process, all of that natural flow so they can come into their own space on that as well. That's my sense that there's going to be almost a reintegration of, revaluing of the way things have been naturally but then now from a more conscious perspective.

Nicholas: Right. Some people might listen to you, someone stuck at the postmodern or the lower levels of development, might listen to what you say and think, "Oh, he's just talking about conservative, back to basics. Men should be men. Women should be women. Discipline, structure, order, Christianity, God, Queen, et cetera, et cetera." You're not really saying that. What's the difference between what you're saying and that?

Peter: I'm saying that there's a place for that but it's temporary. It's a phase of development that's necessary to build certain cognitive emotional capacities in a way that we're pointing to there, the need for order, structure, know your place, natural hierarchy, enables you to stabilize a sense of belonging in the collective. That's why we have societal agreements that we've made with each other because if we didn't, then it becomes very dog eat dog and not everybody but a lot of people would just take for their own ends which is why we have agreements and agreements which are enforced which creates a certain foundation upon which we can continue to grow.

If it was purely only that, then that blocks further developments and becomes suffocating as a channel to blow through on the way to finding your own individual energy and role within that context. It's critical. It's the difference between being an individual who is doing their own thing oblivious to the needs of others to an individual who can find their own creativity and play the game creatively with others within agreed boundaries.

Nicholas: I worried for a long time about what I perceived as the collapse of authority as I was growing up in the 70s and 80s, I observed wherever I looked, things were falling apart. Parents were not being respected, didn't have self-confidence. Teachers couldn't keep control in the classroom. All of the traditional icons were mocked. I experienced that as insecurity and decay. A few years ago, I went around and interviewed a lot of people from very diverse backgrounds about authority.

I asked, "What gives you the right to tell someone else to do something or to inspire someone else to do something," whether it's a teacher, a doctor, a parent, a military officer and so on. It was fascinating because I could almost sense there was an inner compass or a meme, bag of memes here (in the centre of the forehead) and there was a wobble in each one, even though they came from very different backgrounds. It was almost like they were speaking from the same hymn sheet. This is right, this is wrong, this is the map, this is the truth and so on. Now, it was like there's a warp in our system around truth, so this is true, this is not true, this is right, this is not right and this is a healthy boundary. That is the space you're in.

I know what you've been doing with the Wisdom University is looking at how to integrate, how to go beyond the narrow idea of what the science is and answer these questions. Who are we? What's right and what's wrong? What's true, what's false? And so on. Is it clear to you what's emerging? Is there a more effective model of authority and truth coming through?

Peter: What do truth, right and wrong look like from a more transpersonal perspective? That whole concept of natural order is an interesting one because it has a sense that there are some things which are more life affirming than other things. There seems to be beliefs or activities or behaviors that either contribute to the life process or block it in some way. In a way, the discernment at that level is more around whether a way of organizing something, a way of leading, a way of bringing up children or whatever, whether it's supporting the natural life process or whether it's inhibiting the life process. That's what we're looking for the whole time.

To be able to discern in that domain, we need ourselves to have a sense of what that natural life process is. That's, I think, what begins to come online more as we dip into those domains is a deeper feeling for what that is, what those principles are, be it an evolutionary map of the landscape like spiral dynamics which takes us through different stages whereby you can see the children move through different phases of development and support them naturally in that process or be it what they might call sacred or natural geometric principles about how does nature design itself in such a way if you look at a tree or an ecology, that parts are as coherent as possible with the whole.

If you take those principles and apply them to an organization, for example or a community. You take those, the way life seems to do it naturally and then start to do it consciously in terms of our design of schooling, whatever, any domain, then what's likely to happen is that those environments that we create, those habitats that we build are likely to be more life affirming and vitalizing than the box shapes or whatever it is that we create in the moment. Right or wrong, true or false, it's my consciousness in the moment that has a lot to do with what is life affirming or what seems to be most resonant with the life process, based on where a certain collective or individual is in that in that journey.

Nicholas: You were telling me you live in a community. How does that play out there if you have a dispute or if you want to assert a particular position on something?

Peter: It's not so much an intentional community as a neighborhood. It's part of a town neighborhood or a town, so there are 200 households. You have your own house and garden and there's a shared garden, all the cars have to park on the perimeter so you have collective ownership of some of the land around your house and for that you have to make collective decisions.

There's a foundation that, there's a responsibility for representing the voice of the people who live in this neighborhood and who interface with the city council, for example. Really, I've only been there a couple of years and the decision making process is still in evolution. People are just trying to, discover and work out different forms. I think it's been stuck in the past in the consensus-making processes where it's all about having everybody's voices heard but no real direction or boundary setting or taking a decision. It was hard to do for people because of the consciousness but it feels like that's coming into play at the moment, so it's interesting to be following, yes.

Nicholas: Where you are in Holland, there's been a whole series of political murders and, I've forgotten his name. Who's the politician, the tall guy with the blond hair?

Peter: Wilders.

Nicholas: Yes, Wilders. In Holland, you've got in the cities, a very large Muslim population who've moved in in a relatively short space of time. I can see how the values that you talk about are going to be attractive to well educated and liberal minded pluralistic democratic minded people who are aware of different perspectives and who are sensitive and tolerant and open and multiculturally minded.

Obviously, a lot of the cultural center of gravity of the Islamic population who've come into Holland is more towards the absolutistic, authoritarian, patriarchal, and tribal mentality. Now, the challenge is that when those two cultures come together, what happens when you get conflict or disagreement or when one wishes to assert upon the other, what happens? The narrative that comes from Wilders and others is that it's not going to work. We need to either ask those people to leave or train them to be Dutch or at the very least have very strict powerful boundaries.

Do you agree with that because the thing is, I can envisage a really, really happy outcome in which Holland and other European countries are an incubator for an evolution of Islam into the modern world but equally it could all go really badly and end up as an awful bloodbath and a civil war. What's going to guide us towards a happy outcome?

Peter: It's been interesting to track it since I've been here. I've been living here for 12 or 13 years and it's the beginning of the period I was here that you had politicians in the town murdered and then the journalist Theo van Gogh with a very explicit fundamentalist Islamic motive behind it. The Netherlands, having been really frolicking along in this nice fairly protected postmodern mindset that including everybody and being a space for everybody, was really shocked to the core by what happened because where all the talk had been of being tolerant, they were confronting this question of should we tolerate intolerance? If we allow intolerance to have a place, then they'll have that impact on our society. Are there certain rules or values which we should be protecting as a society? Is that going to be exclusive? That whole debate has really been raging since those events happened.

I think the society has really evolved over those years and what happened initially was that we got quite a regression down to a more sense of morality, moral value, order in this society and got this Christian Democrat prime minister Jan Peter Balkenende who was really about values, morals and everything else. The system naturally went back to recover the style of values that have been relativized or swept away by the postmodern mindset saying, "Oh, that's just one kind of thing. There are other qualities, other values," everything else and realizing that this nation also has an identity and a history that is to be honored as well. So that was being recovered, then we got a more progressive Prime Minister and things started to move on.

Yet, still the big challenge is rather leading politicians who most of all, most of whom inhabit this postmodern mindset is being able to engage authentically with the more authoritarian or power-driven value systems that you see coming through, not just the immigrant population but also a lot of the Dutch population, who just haven't been heard over the years. When somebody like Wilders shows up, what he's doing is giving voice to a significant section of the population who haven't been heard by a postmodern elite really that's been off doing its own thing and where the frustration has built up.

I think, like Pim Fortuyn, the analysis and naming of the issue is very valuable to the system. It made people have to confront things in society that they wouldn't just because they didn't have a way to deal with it, would just ignore it. The solution set however is coming from a more ethnocentric perspective. The challenge for the politicians now is to be able to acknowledge the reality that is being reflected by what a Wilders has to say but to come up with a more world-centric response that is the integration of those to the healthy way rather than an exclusionary way.

I think it's going in the right general direction. The other advantage we have of course is when you have political parties like those of Wilders that are built on ethnocentric and power driven consciousness, they start to fall apart which is exactly what's happening now with everybody's infighting in the party, it's disintegrating. This is what happened with these efforts before because they can't hold it together as they're all basically in it for their own means, there are big clashes. In the end, they'll fall apart. They won't be able to maintain the appearance of any sustainable movement.

What is important is that is that the part of society that that is shining a light on continues to be seen by a world-centric politicians and more conscious solutions are found, so that they can have their place and not assume that they can immediately adopt a postmodern consciousness because that's the way it is.

I think there's a lot of innovation going on in that area at the moment over there. Again, that's something the Netherlands might well have in the world is experience from a more conscious perspective of how to work with that rather than an us and them mentality.

Nicholas: What do you see as happening within the Dutch Islamic population? What sort of evolution culturally is going on?

Peter: I don't really have my finger on that pulse so much. In any ethnic group, you have different levels of consciousness. You have your progressive Islamists. You have the more fundamentalists. They've been helping the communities become more stable by using the fathers a lot more in the relationships in that more authoritarian order system. If you want to get to the kids, have the fathers out on the street making sure order is kept so there's security and the community is involved. Also its important to look for opportunities for them to integrate more into the economic life.

Once you get that, then they get involved in the entrepreneurship, science and move away from a closed environment. That's a challenge in the current economic crisis. It's in a way a potent mix that you've got people out of jobs and frustrated and with ethnocentric ways of thinking you very quickly get polarization. We will see how that plays out but the Dutch are doing a pretty good job of it at the moment.

Nicholas: Thank you, Peter. I know you've been doing a lot of work on energetics and consciousness, looking at how fields, both consciousness and energetic fields operate. I'm probably not educated enough to ask you the right questions but what's the cutting edge of that? How do we, say at the very biggest level, how do we create a field within which Western and Global Civilization can be aligned and emerge with the best outcome?

Peter: That's a bigger question and I can't really pretend I have an answer about but ...

Nicholas: I know you've been doing on a small scale.

Peter: Yes. The reason I got to this is because we'd spent quite a while working on large scale projects in organizations, a multi-stakeholder collaboration and using the best of integral approaches and Theory-U and all of these things that basically work on getting a coherent social field or field of relationships between people. We're finding that that becomes incredibly complex when for example, you've got 20 organizations trying to coordinate behind an overarching goal. They all have their own thing and you're trying to keep them connected to each other and it's gotten far too complex. In fact, that whole situation becomes very complex. I always have in the back of my mind, the solution we're looking for is something that's simple, the kind of simplicity is the other side of complexity.

We stopped when we were in the middle of a number of these projects and there must be another way to do this. That's when I started to think more about the whole energetic piece and the way I frame it now is when the reason we have a material architecture, a material dimension to our reality. We were finding that when we get the relational architecture coherent between people that enhances the material, so results get achieved far better in organizations, stuff gets done if the relationships are healthy in the system.

Those two actually lie embedded in what one calls an energetic architecture, so that any system that has a name and a boundary, basically has an energetic field to it. A lot of people are now used to the idea that the human has an energetic dimension to it and Reiki has taken off. You can get it on the street corner now as well. The idea is that if you need to heal yourself then, we send the body life energy and that helps it to heal itself basically. Now, the body is such a complex thing. A cell is far more complex than the rest of our being put together.

How on Earth are we supposed to know exactly what kind of intervention we should make in the body when it's such a complex organism which has been the approach of traditional medicine which goes to the part and tries to fix the part that has caused the problem and that then triggers something else somewhere that wasn't predicted, it triggers something else, it triggers something else.

If we basically trust that the body can heal itself if the stress and blocked energy are removed in the system and it's got enough life force to it that the organs know what they have to do, the cells know what they have to do, if there isn't enough energy flowing around, then we can take that same metaphor as it were and apply it to a social system. Say, you've got a number of players, or organs or organizations in the system that have roles to play to serve people on the planet but if we can create coherent energetic fields around and between those systems that they'll start to play the role they need to play or start to self organize because they know what they have to do fundamentally but with lots of stuff in the way.

I'm in that final year of vocational training in ECOtherapy which is one approach that was originally developed in Germany with something called Resonance Therapy where they were working with forests at a distance that were suffering under acid rain and ozone layer and stuff and finding that if they work the energetic field of the forest at a distance, that it would increase the vitality of the forest, then they have biologists research it and with test trials and everything else including blind controls. It was all proven again by the science that it seems to have an effect.

More recently, it's been applied to organizational systems or human systems more. They've also researched 90 organizations and found that for 12 out of 14 criteria they set up was statistically significant impact where these systems were worked with energetically.

Nicholas: What does that mean, through meditation or getting the people together to do something?

Peter: No. It is working at a distance with the system as well as maintaining contact with the people who were responsible for the system as a whole and working with them to help integrate the energetic information that's coming through. It means you can contact the forest by having a map of it shrunk down to a tiny size but that was a fractal of the bigger system, because it's just in a holographic sense, a smaller version of that bigger reality. You can get in touch with it by just having the small map, as it were, in the same way that healers will get in touch with people at a distance through their name or through a photo or something. We call it a resonator system.

Then, by dowsing, which is simply basically an energetic information register through your body so if you ask a question which is, like muscle testing, you got to push down and like, "Say your name," and if you're strong, you say that, "I'm called something else," and you go weak. That information that's in your body and that's something that's true or not true or more vital as a piece of information or less vital. The same if you're working with a pendulum to dowse. That's just an extension of the movements of your body so if we assume the energetic information we pick up in our body, then you can dowse information about that system once you're in touch with it, so if you're in touch with the forest organization, we have this approach set up an agreed language which reflects our stressed energy in a system, blocked energy, how grounded it is, how much life force there is in the system, how much self organizing capacity the systems is, how much information it has integrated into it.

A number of parameters which measure through dowsing. Say, you go for example, "Okay, how ground given what this systems wants to achieve in the next year, how grounded is it? Zero, 10, 20, 30." Let's say it comes to 30% or something, you have a set of target values for all these different energetic parameters which you are trying to reach, because you think you've got a coherent system. Then you say to the systems in the same way you'd say to a patient in a doctor's surgery or an intelligent doctor would, "What do you need next?" The system will say, "I need grounding." So, "Good, you need grounding. I've got this and this and this symbol and color in my toolkit which tends to help with grounding. Which one of these will be most effective for you?" and you testing them.

Nicholas: Is that all happening remotely or do you need to have the consent and participation of the people in the system?

Peter: What I have is the consent and participation of what we call the steward or the guardian of that system. That could be the head of the department, if it's an organization. That could be in terms of a forest, the warder of the forest but the person or the team of people who are ultimately responsible for that entity, bound with that boundary and that name.

Nicholas: Yes. Does it matter if people believe it because a lot of people would listen to what you're saying and it would just sound magical or unrealistic. Does that matter? Can you do it with ...

Peter: They've got to at least be open to the possibility. For example, last year I was balancing 3,600 hectares of land in the south of the Netherlands and the warden of that land didn't really didn't necessarily believe the theory or how it worked or anything, but he was open enough to be curious, based on the fact that in the past, there are other parks and forest that have benefitted from it, curious enough to say, "Yes, I'm willing to give this a try," then over the year, you notice they get increasingly curious about it.

He doesn't really know the theory of how it works or what's going on but he can feel there's something about it that works. He's been very great supporter of the work, so they have to at least the open to it. The one thing they do have to do, work with affirmations because that's part of the role of the energetic steward or guardian is to be putting an image as it were, into the field or if their desired outcome that what you start to do is then load. It's like think about it as you're beginning to create an increasingly solid photocopy image of your potential future in the field. Say what you're doing is creating increasing wave coherence so it means probability waves into increasing coherence whereby you increase the probability that something's going to cohere enough for it to manifest in the 3D reality.

If they don't do that, then there's very little chance that they'll actually get the results they want. We can get the energetic architecture coherence but if the people in the organization don't do the things they need to do to manifest their goals, then very quickly, the energetic architecture will collapse down as well. It goes hand in hand.

One of the key things I've discovered is you can't really talk about cause and effect at that level. I can't say, "Because we're doing this energetically, it's causing that." They happen together but what we can see in the research is that when there is energetic work done, then the results seem to be more positive than they would be otherwise. It's a new domain but I think it's going to grow very quickly, primarily not just because it's cool but because it increases results.

Nicholas: Yes. I'm open to what you're talking about. I can appreciate that things can happen on that dimension and certainly, you could translate it into more traditional language in terms of confidence, energy, morale, cohesion and so on. I know you're operating on a higher level than that but it can translate it to something that I can understand but I haven't experienced that. Is there a way to experience that, to put it to the test, so that one can apply one's own judgment to that, because if it's true, it's amazing and we all need to do it.

Peter: There's stuff you can look into so you can explore the web site at ecotherapy.org, you can read Hans Andeweg's book, now in English, In Resonance with Nature. There he actually, in In Resonance with Nature, he gives you a number of exercises you can do so you can try it out for yourself. The best way to do it is to have your organization worked with energetically and that's something you really experience how that works in the synchronicity of it.

The other thing we do is we run introductory workshops where you get to feel, you can actually feel the energy, you can feel the energy of the system. It's very simple. It's amazing how simple it is. You can, in one hand feel the energy of your organization, for example, what it feels like now and say you're thinking about a merger, you just put the other organization in the other hand and you start to bring them together. Your body reacts in a certain way, it either relaxes and cheers up or it contracts and that's information.

Nicholas: Yes- and saves an awful lot of money. It would have been interesting to do that regarding the Euro, wouldn't it? Should, we do this.

Should, we have Greece in or not?

Peter: It's just information from another perspective. You still want to do your economics on it. You still want to do all your other due diligence but this is another source of information that you can include on a dashboard. As you say, it's basically free and effortless, it just requires a little bit of openness.

That's also as I started to discover all this, it's part of what I think is emerging in terms of the new civilization. It's far more effortless, far more intuitive, knowing can be instant and decisions are going to be taken very quickly based on and knowing because once you're working in that dimension, space and time collapse so you can check stuff in the future, you can check stuff in the past, you can check it anywhere on the planet. It doesn't matter.

Nicholas: For me, an obvious way to really, really ramp that up would be to integrate it with capitalism because if we see money as energy flowing as a store or representation of human energy flowing into human potential then those people who are stewards of capital whether it be banks or venture capitalists, if you could do the work that you're doing on their investments, then for a hedge fund or for a pension fund or whatever, even just a few percentage points makes a radical difference to the profit. You could actually relatively quickly have a massive impact and make a load of money. Has anyone tried that?

Peter: I think in theory you could but it's like psychics trying to predict the lottery or something. The thing is, anytime we have a project, a balance, we test first from, "Is it okay to balance this?" so you check is this alright to balance? My hunch is that you would only get a "yes" if it's something which is likely to add to the general vitality of the whole so if it was like a lesson was very good reason from it, balancing a project to develop the latest nasty weapon that's going to be used to destroy whatever, then you'd probably get a no unless life had a very weird plan in store.

A colleague was invited to balance an intensive industrial cow farm, a really horrible project. They were really surprised that the assistant said,

"Yes, go ahead and balance it." Half way through, the farmer got the idea that he actually wanted to turn it into an organic farm and everything else. Somewhere in the field was the possibility that this was going to become a life affirming system.

You could work it in the financial sector, particularly if you're interested particularly to look at the ethical finance system. Who knows, maybe it would say, "Yes, go with this Hedge Fund," and then because one of the things we have to be humble about is we just can't know what's in store or what the potential that's in the field. If the system says, "Yes," and you get a yes, then in a way you've got to trust that life has a plan that's going to be for the good of the whole of this thing. Who knows what would happen to that Hedge Fund over time. You see the most amazing synchronicities, developments that happen in these projects when you're working with them that you just couldn't have predicted them from beforehand.

Nicholas: Could we step aside to science? I think science is fantastic and it has brought us from dark and primitive places and transformed our world. I believe it'll continue to do so. Some people just bash science and say, "Oh, it's all bad," or "It's all male dominating patriarchy," and that sort of thing but I think that the way in which we've done it is quite limited and especially when science goes into areas like human behavior, human consciousness, complexity, life and so on, the reductionist predictive falsifiable way of doing it is not so effective.

Could you say a bit about your explorations with the Wisdom University and seeing how to integrate wisdom and complexity into science?

Peter: Yes. For me, I think the best example of the role of science, the positive side and the shadow side is the work of Princeton. When Princeton University engineering department decided to inquire into whether human intention could affect the random generation of numbers of ones and zeros on a computer, because I think the original impulse is they were concerned that pilots when they change their inner state, they would affect the very subtle instruments in the cockpit. They were beginning to pick that up. That was the original impulse, I think. For 28 years, they were doing this research so every time they publish a paper on it, the scientific community would say, "Yes, but you haven't taken into account this." Next they, take that into account. Again, they come up with another. "Oh, you have to do this," and so it went on, millions of these different experiments.

By the time they got to the end, 28 years later, the statistical chance of what they have discovered being chance was one in a billion, okay? That's a scientific, one in a billion is chance that everything they've shown how human intention affects an otherwise random nature of events, the chance of that being a fluke is one in a billion.

Then, in the video, Bob Jahn and Brenda Dunne, who were the primary researchers at Princeton, they called together a compilation of the results including a video. They quote the scientists saying to them, "Even if what you were saying is true, I wouldn't believe it."

Nicholas: Yes, which is faith rather than science.

Peter: You can try to prove it as much as you want but if the concept doesn't resonate with the paradigm, the person, then it's not going to be able to see it, however much evidence you put in front of them. If they can't grock it, if they can't get a sense of it, then it's ... they're still not going to believe it even if it's being proved one in a billion statistically that is true.

I still believe it's very worthwhile continuing to evaluate the impact of your activities in as an integral way as possible which includes a third person analysis but also includes a second person intersubjective exploration and your own inner intuition about things to make it a more integral picture of it.

In the energetic work we always do this thing in pairs or teams so when you get information, you check it with others and you see whether you're getting the same picture or not. That's how science really in its essence should work. It's intersubjective where a number of people corroborate their data and say, "Yeah, we're getting the same figure," or, "a couple of percent off." That kind of thing.

I think it's important for us to take seriously our inquiry into the nature of reality but not to get obsessed with trying to prove things to everybody, because if people aren't open for it, they're not going to believe it anyway, no matter how much data you throw at them.

Nicholas: What is the shadow part of our system? What is the dark unconscious or semiconscious part and how do we bring that into consciousness and heal it in order to liberate our full potential?

Peter: We'll start with what Western Civilization has given us, is the individualization process or in a healthier sense, the individualization process. That step to releasing the creative potential of the individual to find their way, discover the world, find out what their contribution is, add value and be rewarded for that value, that whole piece which is key to growing beyond the just sense of ourselves as embedded in everything else without the individualization piece.

My sense is that the shadow is that what happened when we stuck on the individuated is that rather than transcending and including the sense of the precognitive or instinctive feeling of belonging or being part of the Earth and the human family, we for some reason weren't able to transcend and include that but transcend it and repress it.

As Ken Wilber would say, "We differentiated but then went on to dissociate." Differentiation is very important in it's development. You have to push away from a previous phase to be able to create space to establish the new way of being but then you need to wrap it in again, because that's the pathway, take the essence of the past with you because that's a foundation which you stand on. I think what happens and it's showing up particularly in what we might broadly call Western Civilization but let's say that the world which has embraced industrial development, has pushed away that piece.

That consciousness which we suppressed or push away from in the belief that that will give us greater freedom includes both the relationship to the Earth, the relationship to each other, relationship to our body. Now, they're all the same fundamentally.

I was smiling when you were asking me the question because when you said, "How are we going to reintegrate that?" I think if we can actually begin to see it, remind ourselves that we are the Earth trying to work that out then we in the broader sense of as the Earth is doing it for us right now is what will be confronted with is the result of that repression with the Earth going, "Well, guys, you know." If you choose to ignore this context which you actually belong to and poison your home, as it were, then it's going to come back to you and it's coming back to us in these extreme weather conditions and everything else.

We're being reminded by the mother, as it were, that we depend on this place and we better remember who we are, basically or else, there's no space for us if we're going to abuse the life system that actually gave birth to us and supported us. I think that essentially our job right now is to do whatever healing we need to do in ourselves and collectively to remind ourselves of who we are as the Earth, like it's not we are saving the Earth. No. We are the Earth, trying to rebalance itself. If we can adopt that perspective and it's a very different one that it starts with a basic assumption of relationship and reciprocity rather than one of separation and us doing something to it.

I was saying to the Institute of Social Bankers yesterday. I was saying, "Assume the Earth and the life processes on your side, because it is, that's who you are." You're aligned with the impulse of life and doing things that are going to add vitality to the system as a whole, then you will be greatly supported by everything around you because that's what the system is trying to achieve as well.

There is great pain there as well that we'll have to deal with. Certainly, when I tune into it and do it with groups and people suddenly realize how disrespectful we've been to this place that has actually given birth to us and feeds us, literally every day, not even aware of us walking on a tree as we walk past it or this whole system, it's like we completely forgot that all the trials and tribulations that our physical mothers went through to give birth to us and never said, "Thank you." It's the same thing. When you realize that, then there is some deep healing that needs to go on there but I think that he preconditioned for us where we actually stretch up into the more energetic dimensions of reality and be able to work with that consciously.

One of my favorite quotes is from Ken Wilber where he says, "When the great mother is repressed, the great goddess is concealed." That says, when the great mother is repressed, our relationship to the Earth, or the Earth is repressed in our awareness and our access to the subtle energetic domains of interconnectedness are concealed. We're not going to get access to that until we reintegrate our relationship to the deep feminine you can say, to the Earth, to our bodies and everything else. Yet, what I'm saying is we need access to that energetic dimension to be able to match the complexity of the challenges we're facing.

Nicholas: What does that look like when that's up and running? Where is that working well? Who is a great role model for that?

Peter: Some of the early work that John Seed and Joanna Macy did, they call Deep Ecology. They now call it The Work that Reconnects, I think that had a key piece of that. It's often been translated a little bit too romantically as back to nature romanticism but if you could hold and transfer some personal context and see that the reason you're going back to that level, to that point in our story is to heal and release energy that's being stored there so that it can stream through the system again and give us the energy we need to take the leap. If you can hold it in that perspective, it's extremely important work.

That whole round of deep ecology, I think is a key piece and harmony and has his peace around that. In terms of, we started experiments at the C.H.E. here, we did a PURPLE-RED retreat to look at what would it mean, what would be the Spiral Dynamics code for that interconnectedness and RED being the code for the individuation phase. What would it look like if we were able to from the masculine perspective hold our sense of interrelatedness as we manifest our energy and power?

From the feminine perspective, if the feminine was able to step into its power without fearing that it was going to lose its sense of connectedness that the men and the women split apart to do their work with it and come back together. It was extremely powerful and that's where the natural order insight came.

I don't actually know institutionally to what extent that's being done. In another place, piece of work that's contribution to that is Stanislav Grof's work and the whole Holotropic Breathwork. That's going back to the preconscious phases in our development, even around the birth and what happened in those moments and reintegrating traumas and stuff that happened at that time. That energy is available for us as we move into the transpersonal. Some of the pieces of work I found inspiring to do that piece.

Nicholas: Peter, the things that you and I have been talking about would be, you can imagine it being very popular in New York or San Francisco or in London but obviously, we do live in a globalizing world and it wouldn't necessarily sound the same to a Chinese General or someone working in a factory in Brazil or someone living in a refugee camp in northern Kenya. The reality is the fantastic story that the rest of the world is catching up, technology, ideas, economics have spread around the world. The rest are doing their own thing. With that comes power.

Even for liberal minded people, we still have an imperialist mindset as if we run the world and we're in charge but we're not and ever decreasingly so. What if all of the emerging powers, the Chinese, the Brazilians, the huge number of emerging countries operated a value system which ours was operating at 100 or 50 years ago, materialistic, nationalistic and power based? Maybe we've got no choice. Maybe that's the way it is. If that's true, what can we do to survive it? Is there anything that we can do to help them? It may sound patronizing.

First of all, how can we create a happy outcome? Where you're sitting in the middle of Holland, in the last 150 years, foreign armies have been over that area three times in that period, causing a lot of death and with modern weapons, there are big risks for us having lots of wars. What can we do to have a happy outcome?

Peter: One thing that's important to do is to distinguish between the underlying codes at these phases of developments such as what you're saying about modernity, traditionalism, these are the underlying energies of the developmental phases that people move through, that we've been through in the past. To distinguish those deep codes with the content that people create out of those codes by which I mean, so when we came into this modernist phase, created an industrial age society with all the trappings that we can see around us.

That core code doesn't necessarily mean that we have to create an industrial society the way we have. The essential elements of that code are individual freedom, innovation, progress, growth, a kind of rational exploration of reality. Those can still be honored, I believe by working with technologies and forms that aren't as damaging and destructive to the planet as the ones we have been. We were the early adopters. Western Civilization pioneered that consciousness and they're rapidly learning their lessons so in a way what we have to offer is our humble failings. Turn to these places and go to them and go, "When we were experimenting with this phase, this is what we did and this is where we screwed up. Actually, in our own survival interests, don't do this like we did it and here are some of the leading edge technologies, et cetera that we came up with that maybe are healthy expression that enabled you to move through that phase of development with forms and technologies that are more allied with the life process than the stuff we came up with in our ignorance as pioneers of that consciousness."

That's in a way the position we have in take in it is we tried this, here are our lessons learned. In my sense, we need to make as much of our sustainable technology available as easily as possible to places like China and India and find an economic forum that's healthy but ultimately for our survival, we need those place to adopt these technologies.

Look at China. China's the biggest producer of solar panels anywhere in the world so they're not silly. These people see how we've screwed up. In fact, the Chinese have set up something called the World Cultural Forum as a parallel in a way to the World Economic Forum, saying, "We want to profile China's proud cultural context," and they've asked for example Ervin Laszlo, who's one of the leading system thinkers in the world and really gets the stuff very deeply to help design that forum next year based on the theme of sustainability.

We have stuff to offer and they may well be ahead in a number of different sectors because they'd been doing their homework. The Chinese know, they've seen it on their own doorstep, if they cut down forest, that makes the land less stable. They get floods, landslides and the places start to get devastated which impacts their ability to grow economically and the whole thing.

I think at some level, we can trust the live process and its most global context that we are learning, life is learning or the Earth is learning through us, as all us move forward and as we come up with solutions which are going to be beneficial and help you move through phases of developments in a way that's more aligned with life then I think in a way is our duty to make sure that those are available.

Nicholas: We've seen quite a lot of evidence coming from India, where precisely because they realize that they cannot repeat what we've done, there isn't the money or the resources and because the majority of the population is so very, very, very poor, that kind of austerity and need for simple and cheap solutions is actually driving innovation. I suspect we're going to find that our health systems, for example, which have become completely unwieldy, will actually be reverse engineered from India because they and China will be doing stuff effectively and cheaply which, as ours collapse and become unaffordable, we'll take on.

Peter: Yes, I think so, too.

Nicholas: For anyone that would like to get in touch with you, Peter or follow your work, what's the best web address?

Peter: Very easiest place to go which has links to other stuff as well as my blog which is petermerry.org. Please do get in touch if you want to follow up with, yes.

Nicholas: Fantastic. Thanks very much.

Peter: Thanks for the invitation, Nicholas.

The Future of Europe

A View from Inside the European Union

Helen Titchen Beeth interviewed by Dr Nicholas Beecroft
Helen Titchen Beeth is an evolutionary leader operating at the heart of Europe as a linguist and change consultant in the European Union Commission Headquarters in Brussels. She is a committed European and describes herself as a student and practitioner of individual and collective evolutionary living. In practice this means that she has been learning and experimenting with ways of introducing and scaling up practices that can unleash collective intelligence in large organizations. She is part of a community called Dorpsstraat which is itself an experiment in evolutionary living. Helen describes herself as a committed European but after many years at the heart of EU institutions, she is very much a realist about the major challenges faced by the European institutions.

She believes that is an old world is dying and a new one is emerging. Many of the problems we are experiencing are the death throes of old ways of being, as she puts it, rather like a rooster still running round even though its head has been cut off. We are far from having a new Civilization up and running into which we can leap but there are plenty of people experimenting and innovating.

Europe is much more than its formal institutions. Europe is its land, its people, the communities, the culture, the identities and its deep consciousness. Whilst Helen is very comfortable in many places around the world, she feels fully at home in Europe. At the same time she is both a European, very British and someone who lives on the earth. She believes that our European institutions have done their best to paper over the cracks of past conflict but there remain under the surface deep attachments to our national identities, many shadow parts and healed wounds.

Helen believes that the European experiment in transnational integration as an arena with potential for inventing, discovering and testing patterns that can offer humanity valuable guidance on its road to becoming a sustainable, global society. However she doesn't wear any rose tinted spectacles and is fully aware that the whole system may well unravel and take us to a dark place. In personal terms she walks her talk. She is investing her time and money into building a sustainable community called Dorpsstraat.

However, everything mentioned so far really is superficial. Helen senses of something much deeper is going on. She believes that there is deep shift from the Piscean age to the Aquarian age. This means that the something deep in the structure of the consciousness of our cosmos which shapes both the physical, mental and consciousness structures which we are experiencing. She senses that this is moving to a much more interconnected and flowful state. She observes that many of the structures and institutions which are currently in trouble are those based on an old parent-child model of interaction and those which are emerging tend to take self-organizing and peer-to-peer forms.

One of the deep shifts which she senses is the reemergence and reassertion of the deep feminine within us particularly, of course, in women. She doesn't subscribe to the idea that women have somehow been passive victims in the suppression of the feminine in the last centuries. She believes that women need to show up fully in their deep feminine power and lead rather than try to occupy the space of masculine power, leaving men nowhere to go. As a mother of 2, she observes that her children are experiencing a world very far from that which she grew up in. They are exposed to hugely more influences, potential ideas, role models and opportunities. She leaves the question open as to whether or not they have leapfrogged the egocentric and ethnocentric levels of development into the world-centric level and whether or not they will miss not having a stronger, more deeply rooted national identity. She finds her children provide a mirror for her, often challenging and a source of growth.

Helen thinks that we have lost contact with our ancestral roots so much that we are having to relearn and reinvent them. We don't really know how to live in community and men and women don't really know how to embody the masculine and feminine or to be parents. We try to learn from books, but in the end, we're going to have to learn from experience, wisdom and intuition.

For the interview, Helen wore an Arab headscarf around the neck. I'm not sure whether or not she was conscious of that but, for me, that was highly symbolic. As European Civilization is faltering and going through radical transition, we have within our borders are very fast-growing population from Islamic backgrounds. Many people are predicting that Western Civilization in Europe will simply fade away and be replaced by an Islamic one. She acknowledges that that may happen but senses that the process is more complex than that. Helen discusses the relationship between the masculine and feminine which she observes within Muslim culture. Whatever people's formal belief, she sees huge potential in the people around her from many different backgrounds who now lives in Brussels.

Nicholas: Helen Titchen Beeth. Welcome to the series, Exploring the Future of Western Civilization.

Helen: Thank you, Nick.

Nicholas: Helen lives in Brussels. She is a mother of two children and works in that very rare place, the European Commission headquarters as a linguist and a change consultant. She describes herself as a committed European and a student and practitioner of individual and collective evolutionary living. She believes that the European experiment in transnational integration is an arena in which we're inventing, discovering and testing patterns that can offer humanity valuable guidance on its roads to becoming a sustainable global society.

She has a special interest in practices that can foster the emergence of collective intelligence and collective consciousness in groups and she's currently experimenting with ways of introducing and scaling up those practices in a way that can unleash collective intelligence in large organizations. She says that at the moment, she has a strong call to return to the wild, spending more time in nature and the company of other women.

I've known Helen for a while now and I'm particularly looking forward to asking her all about the big picture and specifically about Europe and how it's developing and also about the feminine, the female, the goddess and the post-feminist and how that fits into the family and our community. Welcome, Helen.

Helen: Thank you.

Nicholas: First off, if I could start with a few questions about Europe. You have a long experience right in the heart of the mechanism of the European Union. What's the state of it currently? Is it in good shape?

Helen: You know it's kind of hard to say. At one level, you wouldn't notice that there was anything wrong. Looking from inside, experiencing it from inside, we're still playing office happily and getting on without procedures and on the other hand of course, when you look out the window and see the very wobbly edifice of the European economy at the moment and the very unreassuring picture of our politicians trying to look as if they know what they're doing, we're in a mess I think.

Nicholas: You're a kind of a catalyst under the surface beavering away, deep away from the headlines trying to bring something great to emerge from it. Are there any sort of green shoots of the new Europe that will arise from the ashes or grow out of this mess?

Helen: I think that a lot that's going on, I think it's important to remember that Europe is not Brussels and it's not the European institutions. It's actually the land mass and the people and the landscapes and the bioregions and the ecosystems and the countries of Europe. It's not the institutions. There I think that there's an incredible amount of an innovation going on and has been for always. I think a lot of innovations has come out of Europe for good and for ill over the centuries and millennia and I think that it's quite possible that that will continue but not necessarily in ways that we find comfortable.

I'm thinking now about, for example, what's happening in Greece, the cradle of Civilization and I think they're busy innovating again, pioneering into the new post-shit-hitting-the-fan era. Well, everybody else in Europe is so kind of keeping a distance from them.

They're boldly innovating because they don't have any choice but otherwise, in terms of innovations happening inside the institutions, I think one of the most promising phenomena that I'm aware of is the fact that the commission is starting to try to listen more to its stakeholders, really listen and come down off its panels and its expertise and just sit around the table with its interlocutors and knock heads together and go, "What do you think we should do next?"

Nicholas: What do you sense is emerging?

Helen: What is emerging is I would say an understanding that the commission's role and the EU's role is not necessarily to think of solutions in its ivory tower and then make laws and impose them on the populace or even just sit around the table as government representatives and bargain and haggle to come up with sub-optimal compromises but the commission has the capacity and the connections to be able to convene Europe-wide conversations all levels of society and all levels of scale from the local and the regional and the national to the European global, in all walks of life, in industry, in science, in research, in technology, in health, in agriculture, in environment all of those different fields.

It's an incredibly complex mess. Of course, it's a mess when you look at it closely because all complex systems are and I think that the men and the women who are trying to make policy are slowly understanding that they're actually dealing with a complex system, not a machine and therefore, we have to roll up our sleeves and get comfortable with not knowing what's going to happen and learning how to co-create together. We're not there yet but that's the movement that I'm seeing.

Nicholas: Yes. I mean that sounds a great evolution if they can hurry that up very quickly.

Helen: Right. The image comes to mind about rooster, that obnoxious rooster that's been running around the farm yard and somebody finally chopped its head off but it hasn't noticed. It's still running around in circles. We'll notice one day that that times have changed but ...

Nicholas: I mean how do you see? Do you have a vision of how it's going to be a really vibrant, dynamic, successful Europe?

Helen: I think that there are a number of things to happen. I think that what I see as potential is not Europe suddenly getting it back together and becoming economically competitive and competing with Brazil and China on their own terms. I've seen that the aging European politicians trying to look cool and it just doesn't work.

There are a number of things I think that we need to do and that we can do. One of them is that we have so many layers of scar tissue in Europe. We've been fighting and killing each other on this territory since the dawn of time and we've been papering over the cracks ever since and that is still festering underneath. I know that every so often, I'm involved in a systemic constellation for example where we're looking to diagnose of what's underneath energetically and systemically what's going on underneath the surface with Europe every time war comes up, every time the war, the holocaust, the enmity between France and Germany and the standoffishness of the UK.

All of these different things, there's a lot there that still needs to be healed. There's a lot of trauma and really, the European institutions were actually created to keep those warring faction apart. "Play nice, guys," and all of the rules are about that but the deep reconciliation and the deep understanding and the appreciation of our national differences is not explicitly on the agenda. That is something I think that needs to change.

One of the places where you see that is in the language wars where even the smaller countries like Malta and Ireland insist that their own, their national languages which even half of the citizens don't necessarily speak must be an official language of the European Union and everything must be translated into those languages at considerable cost and complexity. The French and the Germans, with English gradually getting ascendency, there are lots of sucked teeth around how to strengthen the role of German and French.

I think that a lot of that has to do with the fact that the countries that the member countries of the EU actually feel a little threatened in their identity and when I think about that, I think about the good old days when the European Union was actually called the European community. There's a difference. There's an energetic difference between community and union.

We haven't yet learned how to be the community. Before, all of a sudden, "We have to get our skates on and become a union." I think that that has been probably one of the mistakes that we have made, is not really stopping to think about what is it really that we're doing.

Nicholas: Some people say, "I'm a global citizen" or that the old national boundaries and nation states, national identities are a thing of the past and they will gently fade away because of the communications and technology and the way we're speaking now, the ease of travel and migration and so on will sort of stir us all up into a big global melting pot. Is that not right?

Helen: I don't know. I know that for myself, obviously I have that dreadful heritage of the British sense of humor which means that I'm British for all time and hopelessly lost and I need to get back to my home country in order to have a good laugh but I definitely feel at home in Europe in a way that I don't feel at home elsewhere in the world. It doesn't mean I don't find it beautiful and lovely to be there but I feel at home in Europe.

When I set foot on British soil, it's as if I become solid and three-dimensional in a way just because of the power of the energy, the Earth energy in Britain is just on a different scale for some reason but I feel very much European and I can't speak for the other citizens of the world but I feel like an inhabitant of the Earth definitely but rooted in a particular part of the world.

I was born in the UK and I've spent my formative years there. I remember still thinking how lucky it was that I was born in the best country in the world. That was to give an example of my education but that was back in the 60's and the 70's of course. My children were born in Brussels but they were born to a Swedish father and a British mother in a country that speaks Flemish and French and German and they go to one of the European schools in Brussels where they're in the Swedish language section with English as their second language.

My son speaks six languages. My daughter speaks four languages. When they go to Sweden, they're foreign. When they go to Britain, they're foreign.

Where they live in Belgium, they're foreign so that is a real question I have. If the normal development of a human being goes from egocentric to ethnocentric to worldcentric, then are my children going to be missing a stage or have they found other peers to belong to? We put them in the European school so they'd be with all the other third culture kids who are in the same boat as they are. There is a community of individuals who aren't rooted in a place and yet most of the rest of us still are born, grow up, grow old and die within a very small radius of where they were born.

Nicholas: I've been wondering about the way the euro is going. Obviously, there are lots of potential outcomes but if it's going to work, it seems that if it's going to survive, it seems that there's going to have to be a lot more central control and a lot more common political structures and political consensus and similar mechanisms and more top down and heavy and inevitably the drivers of that are going to be the more successful countries. Those are the more disciplined and more prosperous countries, Germany being the obvious one but the others like the Danes and the Finns and the Dutch and so on.

The countries who are going to be most subject to the thumbscrews are going to be the obvious ones, the Southern countries and it's very non politically correct to say so but in those countries, it's endemic in their culture that there are more bending of the rules and go for gray rather than black and white and there's no way they're going to like to be screwed down really hard by the Germans and the others. It seems to me that that's like petrol and a match for their nationalisms.

You can already see it in Greece with them having pictures of Angela Merkel in a Nazi uniform but it seems to me like that's just the beginning. It could get a lot uglier quite quickly. Is there any way to stop that from unleashing or to make a positive thing of that?

Helen: Barring a miracle and yet a miracle would be completely possible but it requires our politicians to tell the truth which is, "We don't know what the fuck to do. We don't." We've already thrown, what, two, three, four times the entire annual budget of the EU this year trying to bailout banks and it's not making any difference at all so to be honest, I don't really think that this is about the euro and I don't think it's about Western Civilization either. I think it's something bigger going on, Nick.

There's something, again, there's something going on under the surface but all of this is the symptom and we're seeing the old and the new together in the same space. I think there is a lot of experimentation going on. I think very strongly for example of the whole peer-to-peer movement and all of the ways that that is manifesting itself. There's a huge divergence or dissensus and people are experimenting wildly with so many different ways of living and being that's a new system. You can't call it a system yet because it's not in place yet.

I think it was Peter, wasn't it Peter Merry who you spoke to last week who said, "Actually, it's dead already." We're walking around in our zombie suits pretending that everything is alright and that's what's happening with the Euro. That's what's happening with the banks. It's what's happening with the EU at the moment. It's like men and women are trapped inside this kind of robot suits that are going through the motions of the way they've always done things and we need to free ourselves and get out of these mechanisms. That's what I see.

I see it certainly in the men and women walking inside the European Commission but I also see it in society at large, is we are trapped by our conditioning inside the old structures. We cannot imagine life being any other way than it is. When I say that I'm going back to the wilds, that's really what I mean, is can I shed my conditioning just bit by bit and still function in those corridors, among those men and women as a liberated soul in general, evolutionary troublemaker or is the only way to just get the hell out of there and go and knit my own clothes somewhere?

Nicholas: Yes. Someone was telling me last week that the bankers in London are buying defensible land which just sounds very medieval, expecting ...

Helen: Very masculine.

Nicholas: It is. They're expecting trouble and ...

Helen: Yes. Well, I mean I've been buying not defensible land but land that was calling to be stewarded in a different way and I'm investing ... it's like I'm getting my money out of the banks. I'm not even waiting to invest it in my children's education I'm afraid because I think the next few years are going to be tough and so I'm investing my money now in making my life money proof and not only mine but also a few other people because I can't see this ending well.

We've been tapering over the cracks way too long and we've been in denial for the last what, 20, 30, 40 years. Things could have gone differently I think if we paid attention in the 70's with the first oil crisis but instead, we just drilled and drilled and burned and burned and went superficial and ...

Nicholas: Helen, (laughing) this was meant to be upbeat and positive!

Helen: It is. It is but in the meantime ...

Nicholas: No, I totally agree with you. I sense all of that too but of course I know that you're not just a doom-and-gloom-monger. You know those risks are there and you know there are those dark clouds but do you see any signs or do you sense what's emerging? What's coming next, a more positive vision, a more positive future? Are there seeds that are taking root?

Helen: Again, I don't see. I sense and this is really where the feminine work comes in I guess, is I sense the certain patterns of unmanifest potential. Some of them are desirable and some aren't. The doom-and-gloom scenario where we just all slide off the cliff tearing each other's eyes out and fighting each other and trying to survive and having to have defensible land just to put up walls and guns and it's quite a Mad Max scenario, I'm prepared to put my life on the line in order to create an alternative to that scenario.

Really what I see is potential because of my own experience, is the humanity has reached a stage now where we are capable of overcoming our basic psychology, of transcending on the conscious kind of dumb mechanisms that have us projecting on each other and not recognizing

116

our own shadow, not recognizing our own egoic contractions and defensiveness. All of those things. I see a huge potential for us to actually get it for ourselves and I see us doing that collectively. That's one piece, is learning to live together peacefully and creatively.

One of the places where I see people learning that is for example in the Occupy Movement. We've got a way to go yet but that's something that I'm working quite intentionally with myself, experimenting and also writing on that and conducting kind of large scale experiments but still quite small obviously but over the long haul.

The other thing which might sound a bit stranger is that humanity actually has potential. Human beings have the potential to co-create with nature in ways that we haven't done before, in ways that we've not known we could and that has to do with our basic nature of having free will in a way that nature doesn't and yet we are part of nature and we can communicate with nature but it's got to occur to us. I think we're slightly held back by our own understanding of the scientific paradigm from doing that but there are enough sort of non-scientific wackos out there like me who just go ahead and do it because I've not read that it's impossible.

Nicholas: Yes. You're putting a few tantalizing hints there. What do you sense is the deeper underlying shift that's going on?

Helen: Kind of the epochal shift from what was known as the Piscean era which was the last 3,000 years or so shifting to the age of Aquarius, the Aquarian era. It's the whole of the cosmos; at the heart of everything, there's the first impulse and I mean this is described by ... in the Tibetan cosmology, they described this as well. There's a huge, big kind of void that is the root and the the ground of all it is.

Again, even the Bible in the creation, God moves across the faces of water and that's the first movement which has a particular pulse like God's heartbeat and everything basically coalesces around this deep underlying pulse and that's how matter forms, how structures form, how Civilizations form. Everything that you see around you are, certainly in terms of our Civilization, our economy, our religion, our education, our politics, our institutions, everything is a manifestation or a response to that basic impulse.

For the last 3,000 years or more, it's been basically a parent-child pattern so there's this hierarchy. There's a power differential whether it's the God, the father and we're the children. We either worship nature or we subdue it. There's always this power of thing. It's transactional and I see it all over again with the parent-child relations and I see it wherever I look. There's that unconscious stuff going on and the new impulse. I mean that's shifted now. That's gone. That's no longer what's happening in the heart of the universe now.

Instead, we've got this different impulse but it's not been going long enough yet for the structures to have arisen but we're starting to sense the patterns and we're starting to see them emerging, the hints. Again, we have the peer-to-peer movement where we're co-creating with each other. It's a natural manifestation of that shift.

The other one I think for example are that the art of hosting meaningful conversations, this pattern of bringing people together to talk and to co-create through conversations where everybody is equal and nobody is the boss and yet together, we come up with new wise decisions and wise actions. People actually see what needs doing and they do it without having a committee or bossing each other around or any one clear person arising as the dominant chimpanzee and the pack but the leadership moves where it's needed depending on the skills called into to place. That's a whole new different paradigm.

That's where we are called to co-create with God in a way. We're a part of that mechanism provided that we now grow up and learn how to stand on our own two feet as adults rather than playing either the parent or the child. That's the learning that we have to do now, is basically what does it mean to actually be an adult of this species?

Nicholas: What does it mean to be an adult of this species?

Helen: Damned, if I know, I'm still learning but it's actually very nice I feel. You could say that there's also a masculine part and a feminine part in all of this and I certainly can't speak for the masculine part. Maybe you can do that in a bit but the feminine part, what I'm learning is that being an adult means standing up for it being okay for me to do whatever I feel like doing now and now and now, just really following my natural flow as a natural human being part of nature.

Nicholas: Helen, you're saying that you've been feeling more empowered to tune in to your sensing, your will, your intuition of knowing what's next and living more according to that but of course you do a nine to five job with rules and other people telling you what to do. How does that all fit together?

Helen: Well, actually what's really interesting about it, I mean it isn't like that at all. There's nobody who's expecting me to stand to attention. As long as I am in my power, I can show up at 10:00 in the morning and say, "Hi, guys. I didn't feel like coming in at nine. I'm not going home early as well." They'll go, "Oh, sure. No problem, fine."

There's something about we get what we expect so if we project the terrifying paternal authority onto our employer, whoever that is or a hierarchical superior, we make ourselves small and we're acting out of our childhood trauma very often. Really it makes us believe really to think that we are so smart as a species in going for a gratification in our comfort, and our convenience and yet we haven't come to grips at all with our own inner demons.

We're just so busy with the outside world that we haven't understood how much of that we're actually just projecting from our own inner disowned bits and pieces out onto the world which is not coming on to that fact at all so it's very, very liberating to just kind of collapse in a heap and recognize all of this stuff that we thought we hated about ourselves or we're ashamed of and to just be able to bring it all back into the fold again, just be ... let it all hang out. Be who you are and be fine with that because everyone else is.

Nicholas: Does it get you in trouble speaking like this?

Helen: Never. You'd think it must do but it doesn't because I'm speaking as a human being and I'm speaking to other human beings. When you come from that place, it's like people almost have no choice but to respond from there as well so it's a really sneaky thing to do.

Nicholas: Do you not find that defenses come up or all the reasons why you can't do that come up?

Helen: Not the reasons why I can't do it. The reasons why they can't do it, yes. But that doesn't alter my freedom. I practiced Buddhism for a good seven years a while back so I studied and practiced quite intensively and particularly the Mahayana and the Vajrayana tradition are absolutely beautiful. I always think of the Dalai Lama saying, "Your enemy is your best teacher because only from your enemy can you learn true tolerance and true patience," which is true. It's the people who press your buttons the worst do you have the most to teach you. They have these wonderful statements like, "Give away all victory and just take on all defeat." If anyone comes at you or guns blazing and blames you, just go, "Yes, alright. I'm so sorry." You're still there afterwards.

Nicholas: It's very patronizing to ask you this question because you're a woman and therefore women know about their family and cooking and child rearing. Can I do that?

Helen: Yes!

Nicholas: With shift that you're talking about, the changes and collective wisdom and deep intelligence, how's that going to play out in the family in a home setting?

Helen: I think one of the really important things to understand is again, it's not part of our real shared culture but it needs to be, is how children develop. In the old days, children were just treated like little adults, even portraits just look like these pinched little adults and I think in a way, certainly in some cultures, we've gone too far the other way. We spoil our children rotten and there's a lot that we unconsciously pass on to our children because we cannot process our own childhood stuff.

What I'm noticing now particularly in my relationship with my own children is that they're holding up mirror to me which a real, real invitation. I mean either I can get stinky and ball at them for being cheeky or I can go, "Shit, you're right. Yeah." My son has a radar and he has a bullshitometer that is just so spot-on and he just holds up every single bit of my hypocrisy. I get it in the neck and so ... what do I do with that?

What do I do with that? There are many ways I think with which I see that my children are ... and I think when I look around their friends as well, our young people are coming from a very, very different place than we were. They have many more influences than we do and many more choices than we do but they have a whole wide range of choices, examples and role models that they can choose from so growing up today is not anything like it was when we were young, Nick.

My kids are now 16, twins. They're 16 years old now so when I see people go, "Oh, God. That must have been so dreadful. How awful and it's so difficult," but actually it's been an absolute joy. I mean obviously, they've had moments of discomfort but for me, I mean all I've had to do is just hold space for their unfolding maybe and just witness them and stick a sock in my mouth anytime I wanted to criticize or advise or any of those things because if they need, they want to know something, they'll ask.

I do think that in future, I mean they say it takes a village to raise a child and I would love to see us much more collectively relating at the community to the community's children.

Nicholas: Yes. Well, there's a whole lot of fear about that, isn't there?

Helen: ... a whole lot of fear, did you say?

Nicholas: Yes, in Britain, a culture of ...

Helen: Right. That's ... all these sexual perverts.

Nicholas: That's right. Everyone is a pedophile unless proven otherwise.

Helen: Doesn't that say something huge about disconnect in us around our own sexuality? It's just something else. It's a taboo that needs to be brought out in the closet and healed. I mean so what are we trying to do? We're trying to control it. We're trying to put laws on things and get stricter and stricter and stricter. It's the same what we're trying to do with the Euro and this is what it looks like when you're trying to hold it together and it's trying to fall into pieces. It's the same pattern.

Nicholas: How does that apply to children and pedophilia or sexuality though?

Helen: The way that we're trying to rule ourselves of and protect ourselves and you're not allowed to talk to children. You're not allowed to touch children because it will be misunderstood. Children are not allowed to strip off their clothes and run naked into the fountains because some old guy might get a hard on. I mean, sorry but ... so what?

We don't have to act on our urges of course and our impulses but it needs to be dealt with because each of these pedophiles is in fact a symptom. They are a victim of our unhealthy attitudes towards our sexuality. It's one of the things that occurred to me to say again about Europe, is that in America, in New Zealand, in Australia, in South America, in all these different places, there are the aboriginal community and the newcomers. But in Europe, we are the aboriginal people of Europe but somehow lost our connection to our deepest culture, to our aboriginal roots.

That, I think we have this veneer of Civilization and we don't have anywhere to look for the deep wisdom because our shamans have not evolved. They've not kind of hidden away and protected themselves from the invader. They've just ceased to be and so many of our deepest roots are no longer connected to our society and so, the whole business of raising children is not as natural to us. We have to read "How to do it" from Dr. Spock. It's not as natural to us as it used to be and so that's part of the challenge now for example for the feminine and to the women, is going back deeply into our primal knowing in a way, our bodily visceral knowing of how to live in accord with nature and with our nature and how to bring that forth into the social space.

That's going to require some collective feminine leadership. We have been complaining for years about how men have had it all their own way and it's a man's world and yet the masculine cannot be held fully responsible for the absence of the feminine. We have to show up. I mean obviously, there's also still a great deal of problem around underground trauma well around the witch burnings and all of that trauma, which women still carry.

Nicholas: Well, you mean Christians, Christianity burned the pagan people.

Helen: Exactly. The wise women, the medicine women. The strong women, the attractive women, the women who were 'dangerous,' but it's safe now. Certainly, in Western Civilization, nobody is going to get burned for standing up. We have to learn to speak now, to speak our truth and speak what we know.

Nicholas: Actually, that's oddly that's a link in to something I wanted to ask you because I see that you're wearing an Arab head dress. Is that right?

Helen: Yes.

Nicholas: How symbolic that you are sitting in the center of Europe as a woman talking about going back to the deep feminine and you're wearing an Arab, Muslim, Middle Eastern male head scarf around your shoulders and of course the city that you're sitting in is, I think, 40% immigrant Muslim, something like that, and growing fast? We don't live in a vacuum. Western Civilization and Europe, all the things we've been talking about that don't live in a vacuum and the scarf that you're wearing represents to a degree that those people and also on a global perspective, the massive transition the Islam is having and the dimensions you're talking about between masculine and feminine are playing out in that as well, aren't they?

Any comments on that? The apocalyptic scenario is that as the old European structures are falling apart as we're in a real mess with who we are and even down to the core of family and being and spirits and truth and so on, we have, in our midst, a very fast growing population of people who, of course they're diverse and they don't all come from one sort of narrow mindset but, they are linked to a group which has got very strong absolutistic and patriarchal mentality, quite a tribal mentality and clearly, a willingness to fight, kill and die. The safety you talked about of being free to say what you like, that's OK case as long as you don't criticize that way of thinking and if you do, you're in deep trouble. How does that sit with everything we've been talking about?

Helen: It's funny as you're speaking, I think about all of them, the different races and different shapes and sizes of people that I come across for example on the metro, when I'm traveling in the metro and whatever they believe, I see the capacity for warmth, love, generosity, caring and a lot of the absolutism also comes from fear and it comes from the imbalance between the masculine and the feminine somehow.

I think in the more heavily fundamentalist societies, there is a strong imbalance between the women and the men. Many other Islamic societies which are a more moderate have a very good understanding between men and women and I'm not sure that the kind of radical feminism of some of western societies necessarily either healthy or helpful.

My inquiry is really about what does the society look like where men and women are in a healthy relationship to each other. It's like I don't think we know anymore.

Certainly, I mean I've seen and experienced a kind of a trajectory as a woman. I've, over the last what, five to 10 years, I've kind of descended into my body and incarnated a little bit more in my body and spent more time with women and less time with men and collectively just exploring what is the healthy feminine? We're now getting to the stage where we're starting to go "OK, now, we have a sense of what a healthy feminine is and how us, women, can be healthy and support each other?"

Now, what happens when we come to be together with men? One of the things that I haven't really recognized or understood was what it's like for men because it's like asking a fish what's it like in water but really, really understanding how they don't have much choice in the matter always having to be in competition with each other.

For example, in a tribe, you can't just all stick around like dudes togeth-er and be just bond as equals and brothers because the guy at the top is constantly having to fend off attacks and challenges. There's always this stuff going on. It's just part of what it is to be masculine whereas the women could say, "Why don't we sit in circle and talk about it?" There's this huge difference.

I had a lovely experience the other week where we were actually doing that. We had the women circle and the men have their fire and they were sitting around that fire. We're all both outside in nature and the women were around their circle and the men were around that fire. We wanted to come together to find a way of coming together in a natural way. It was like whatever we did, it was either the women had to come together on the men's terms and we say, "We've been doing that the past 3,000 years, forget it," or the men would have to come together on the women's terms and they go, "No, that's not the way men do it. We don't just sit in circle. No. It's not what we do." It's like, so how do we do this? How do we do this? In the end, we just let it happen in a wonderful, in a way.

The first thing that we discovered was that the men had their fire and the women, we had our fire but actually we let our fire go out because we didn't want to be sitting around the fire because we wanted to be close to each other and the fire got in the way so the fire went out and then it started getting cold and dark and we'd like to have our fire back. Of course, we're perfectly capable of lighting a fire but we decided that what we wanted to do was we want to ask the men, "Please, we let our fire go out. Would you please light it for us?" and men were delighted. In fact, we've forgotten how that the woman's strength is our vulnerability.

The women today hate batting their eyelids and being helpless and yet when the woman shows up in her masculine power, what the fuck is a man supposed to do? It's like they've got no ground to stand on, it's almost as if a man cannot be in his power if I'm in his power so that if I'm in my power, the feminine power which is much more vulnerable. Mine is to open and surrender and yours is you better not drop me so when I am in that vulnerable space, it's an instant invitation, spontane-ous invitation to the man to step into his power.

The women have a lot more power in this whole thing than we realize because if we're occupying your space, we don't leave you any room so you'd go off and act out in all sorts of horrible ways because we're out of balance. So there's a lot of experimentations to do but what we've discovered is that sure, it's hard to just surrender when you're not sure if the person's going to drop you but if we don't, it's very hard for a man to be in his power if he's getting a whole lot of signals from a woman that she doesn't trust him so that's the gift that we have to make now, is about how to trust, is to show up in our vulnerability. That's a huge act of leadership to do that.

One of the things that we've noticed is that actually women bounce so even if we get dropped, we bounce but the thing that allows us to bounce is other women so it's learning to be in a support network of women is what makes that possible. So how neat is that?

Nicholas: Yes. It's amazing to listen to you, Helen. You have a huge richness of experience there. So, Helen, thank you so much for what was a really rich and deep conversation and I think there's several books and speeches and a huge amount of wisdom in there which I really would like to see you share.

Helen: Well, I think I shall call you up and interview you.

Nicholas: That'd be a great pleasure, it'd be about time.

Helen: After all of the wonderful experiences that you've had from a lot of the conversations that you had and all of that learning, it would be very interesting to hear how that's all amalgamated in your life and work.

Nicholas: Fantastic. Very finally, Helen, if someone would like to get in touch or follow your work, what's the best web address for that?

Helen: My writings appear on my blog which is Integral Yeshe, http://iyeshe.wordpress.com. I also do a blog called Aquarian Conversations which is actually channel work and that's, http://aquarian conversations.wordpress.com. That's really mainly about this whole transition between the Piscean and the Aquarian era and what's showing up from the norm manifests realms, about that. It's not something I tend to write on my CV. Since it's you Nick, I'll make exception. Otherwise, there's the Dorpsstraat blog which is where I'm chronicling our adventure in money-proofing our lives which is an experiment in eco-building and permaculture and community living in relationship to a place which is also sensing different aspects of our shared future. http://dorpsstraat.wordpress.com

Nicholas: Great. Thanks very much, Helen.

Ending the Culture War

A Devoted Conservative and a Die-hard Liberal Make Friends

Professor Phil Neisser and Jacob Hess interviewed by Dr Nicholas Beecroft

"You're not as crazy as I thought. (but you're still wrong) Conversations between a Devoted Conservative and a Die-Hard Liberal" by Phil Neisser and Jacob Hess is an inspiring attempt by its authors to show how we can move beyond the energy sapping conflict between left and right, conservative and liberal and other political polarities. They demonstrate that at the very least it's possible for liberals and conservatives to come to a position of mutual understanding and respect. They show that it is possible for us to integrate the best, the healthy strands of different political dimensions into an integrated whole.

Phil describes himself as a leftist and a liberal (in the American sense of the word) and Jacob is a Christian Conservative and proud Mormon. They had both grown tired of the culture wars in which the left and right have become ever more polarized, sometimes to the degree of mutual hatred and always to the detriment of America. Similar processes are found around the world. They set about the disciplined process of identifying the many subjects about which they had strongly opposing views and, one by one, they patiently listened to one another until they fully understood each other's positions.

The subject which they found most contentious was the case for gay marriage. We took that as a case example in which each set out their view and then described the process they went through. In fact, as the interviewer, I had quite a hard job to try to stimulate any tension, emotional triggers or conflict as a way of demonstrating their positions and original polarity. This is because they've done such a good job of working through the issue that they can now very comfortably discuss it in a very mature, reasoned, nuanced way in which they fully respect the position of the other. They could even see some ways forward on the subject which may offer breakthrough.

I invited them to explore the challenges faced by the West, particularly Europe, as a result of high levels of immigration of Muslims at a time when Islam is going through a very turbulent phase of its adaptation to the modern world. As a Mormon, Jacob is a member of a religious minority which is quite traditional and conservative, yet successful as living as prosperous, democratic, patriotic Americans. I asked him whether there were any lessons for Muslims in Europe as to how best to make a success of integrating into Western society without compromising their religion and values. He said that Mormons had suffered a great deal of persecution both historically and currently and he felt that Christians and Mormons in particular have a lot in common with Muslims. If anything, he felt that globally that the fault line was not between Christians and Muslims but rather between religious people and secular people. He felt that one of the key things in enabling successful integration is to see the humanity in the person and group with which one does not agree. He gave examples of that and showed how it had softened his position on many subjects whilst still remaining true to himself and his beliefs.

I asked Phil to say how he navigates between being open, tolerant and accepting of diversity whilst also being willing to assert some values as better than others. He draws the line at the use of coercion and violence. He believes that people should be free to live as they choose including living according to their religious beliefs but that they should not be permitted to impose those upon others. We discussed the reluctance of some of us to assert our values for fear of being accused of being racist, Islamophobic or similar.

Jacob described how he, as a Mormon, has learned to have great self-confidence in asserting his beliefs as the truth. He spent 2 years traveling around Brazil knocking on doors to share his truth. He believes that everybody should be confident to do that as well as also being free to disagree. In fact, that was one of the common themes throughout the conversation that a healthy political culture needs us to enshrine the willingness to disagree. Having said that, there are some things upon which we need to agree in order to live together as one community. Jacob gave a very practical example of a swimming pool in his community which is largely Mormon. The majority of the community will

THE FUTURE OF WESTERN CIVILIZATION

vehemently against the use of the pool on a Sunday, the Sabbath. The minority were determined to use the pool on a Sunday as an expression of their freedom and rights. They managed to find a compromise through dialogue which enabled both sets of people to retain their own beliefs and protect their way of life.

They finished off by saying how the lessons from their conversations could be scaled up to improve our political culture and institutions.

Phil Neisser teaches political theory at the State University of New York at Potsdam, where he also serves as the Associate Dean of Arts and Sciences. Neisser earned his M.A at Georgetown University and his Ph.D. at the University of Massachusetts at Amherst. He is the author of United We Fall: Ending America's Love Affair with the Political Center (Praeger, 2008), co-editor of Tales of the State: Narrative in Contemporary U.S. Politics and Public Policy (1997), and the author of essays and book chapters on a variety of subjects. And in the year 2000 he received a SUNY Potsdam Presidential Award for Excellence in Teaching.

Visit www.philneisser.com

After graduating from Brigham Young University as psychology department valedictorian, Jacob Hess was admitted to the doctoral program at the University of Illinois, Urbana-Champaign. There, he was invited by the UIUC Program on Intergroup Relations to help develop and co-facilitate a liberal-conservative dialogue course for undergraduates, the first of its kind in the nation. Jacob also joined Nathan Todd in interview research comparing narratives of liberal and conservative citizens. After completing his Ph.D. dissertation research on long-term depression treatment outcomes in 2009, Jacob has worked as research director at Utah Youth Village, a non-profit for abused children in the Rocky Mountain region.

Nicholas: Phil Neisser and Jacob Hess, welcome to the series, "Exploring the Future of Western Civilization."

Phil: Thank you, Nick.

Jacob: Thank you.

Phil: Good to be here.

Nicholas: I'm going to take advantage of both of you being here to get each of you to introduce the other. So Phil, would you mind introducing Jacob, briefly?

Phil: Nick, this is Jacob, now a good friend of mine after talking for two years and getting to know him. He lives in Utah, and part time research director at a not-for-profit that helps abused and troubled children, recently completed his PhD in social psychology, and a great listener and a great person.

Nicholas: Fantastic! Jacob, would you mind introducing Phil?

Jacob: Thank you, Phil. This is Dr. Phil Neisser. I met him at a conference several years ago, and he had just finished publishing a book called *United We Fall*, which argues that Americans are losing the capacity to disagree with each other in healthy ways. It's a fantastic book, and we got talking about writing another book together, which we'll talk about. I can't say enough good about Phil. I love to tell my religious friends what a good man, good moral man this atheist guy is, it throws them off their world view a little bit. Phil has taught me a lot about a lot of things.

Phil: Thank you.

Nicholas: Fantastic! What job do you do, Jacob?

Jacob: I'm starting a nonprofit right now, but I work as a researcher and a writer.

Nicholas: And you also work with children, I understand?

Jacob: Yes. Alternative treatments for depression, is the focus of my research. A more holistic, comprehensive approach.

Nicholas: Great! Phil, you're a professor of politics?

Phil: Yes. I teach political theory at State University of New York at

Potsdam, which is the far northern reaches of New York State near Canada. I'm the chair of the department, and I'm part time Associate Dean of Arts and Sciences, so I haven't been teaching as much lately. I have overall been teaching political theory for about 25 years.

Nicholas: Great. The reason that we're speaking is because of the book written by these two guys, "*You're Not as Crazy as I Thought (But You're Still Wrong)*." Conservative one way, liberal the other. And you can see I've put a couple of polarizing people behind me. (Pictures of the Dalai Lama and Margaret Thatcher) Could you say, what is this book about and why is this book necessary?

Phil: I think the book demonstrates a better kind of politics, in which people don't compromise on their principles, yet they still listen to each other. Jacob and I are not the only ones doing this. There is a movement kind of underneath the radar in this direction, and the movement is needed because the politics that we have is teaching us falsehoods about each other, is driving wedges between people, and it is failing us when it comes to addressing policy problems, understanding the complexities of the dilemmas we deal with, and so on. It's just turning us off from each other and making us become enemies. We can do better, and the book is an attempt to show, yes, we can do better. Jacob, how's that?

Jacob: I agree. I've become more of a hedonist since writing this book with Phil. When people ask me why, why did we write this book, why are we suggesting that people try this? My answer is, it's really fun! And when you endlessly try to debate and proselytize and persuade, not only are you not learning things, but it's not very enjoyable. This is just so mind-blowingly fun to put your stuff up out there and be open, and learn things you didn't learn before. So that's why I'm sharing it.

Nicholas: Great! I think it would be good from a tribal perspective to get you both to show your tribal credentials. From my understanding of reading your book, Phil, you consider yourself to be a leftist, or liberal?

Phil: Yes. I define as liberal in the American political language. I'm to the left of liberal. I distinguish between leftists and liberals on some issues. Maybe that's a little European and lost on some Americans. I'm definitely to the left of center on economics, on social issues and so forth, absolutely. Sometimes I vote for the Democratic party reluctantly because they're not left-wing enough, let's put it like that.

Nicholas: Oh, okay. So if you were in England, you'd be a Labour party supporter.

Phil: Yes, at least. Labour party, Green party.

Nicholas: Or more.

Phil: Yes.

Nicholas: So are you a liberal as well? Does that kind of overlap with being ... Because liberal could mean Libertarian or-

Phil: Right. In the European context, liberal could mean Libertarian and Americans don't think of it that way. In a way, Franklin Roosevelt stole the word and changed it, and so for Americans, liberal means in favor of government regulation of corporations and the economy.

Nicholas: Great. Thanks.

Phil: Yes.

Nicholas: And Jacob, can you, so the people reading know roughly where you're coming from, from a political tribal perspective, can you locate yourself?

Jacob: Sure. Let me say first though, I've come to believe that everyone has a liberal and a conservative dimension. I don't know anyone that wants to keep everything the same. I don't know anyone that actually wants to change everything. So there's a healthy tension here, right? There are some things that I have come to see, to have similar questions as Phil on the role of big business, and power structures. I definitely do in this tension fall along the conservative continuum, where there are things that I want to keep the same that Phil wants to question, and I'm a card-carrying Latter Day Saint; Mormon is the nickname.

Nicholas: Yes.

Jacob: And Mormons span the political spectrum, but yes, I'm deeply religious and conservative in almost all the ways you think of conservative.

Nicholas: Great. So sort of low-tax, small states, big defense, social conservative?

Jacob: Yes.

Nicholas: Great. I know that the reason that you met was because you went to the, is it called the National Center for Dialogue?

Jacob: Dialogue and Deliberation, yes. Sandy Heierbacher started it back in Pennsylvania, and that's where we met.

Nicholas: So, if you were both polarized tribal warriors in the culture war, you wouldn't possibly have considered doing that. So maybe Jacob first, what was it that made you decide to engage with an organization that's based around bringing people together in dialogue?

Jacob: I went to graduate school, Nick, and I was the conservative kid in a very liberal psychology department, a PhD program. I was shy, I had no interest in debating everyone and trying to convince them of how I saw the world, so I just shut up for the first couple of years. Then I took a dialogue class and I realized, hey, there's an alternative to just shutting up or debating. I fell in love. It was love at first sight. I co-facilitated a dialogue between Mormon friends and friends from the gay and lesbian community. That was my first attempt to co-facilitate. It eventually led to a class, and I was presenting results on the class when I met Phil. So I went to that conference as a venue to share results from a Liberal-Conservative Dialogue course that I had been involved in.

Nicholas: And Phil, likewise, if you were just a kind of radical leftist ideologue, you wouldn't bother to talk to a conservative. What drew you to do that?

Phil: I guess your premise, I would question it a little bit, because I think a lot of liberals and leftists are pro-dialogue, though not as much as I'd like it to be. There's definitely those ideologues who just aren't. Or, let's put it this way. In many extreme left-wing circles, there's been a lot of sectarians where people enjoy dialogue, but in order to factionalize and tear each other apart, and each claim they know Marx or whatever, we're an argumentative bunch, for good and bad. Otherwise, I'd say it's my nature just as a person.

So while I'm liberal and leftist on the issues, it's my nature. Also, I had some great teachers in college and in grad school who assigned me conservative texts. I read them. I read George Gilder. I read Burke and other famous conservatives. Charles Murray, one of my arch opponents, I've read several of his books, I've assigned some to my students. I saw a value in reading them, and I saw some truth in those pages. I said, well, I guess it's worth talking to conservatives.

Nicholas: Great. So having established the territory, what I'd really like to do is pour on a load of petrol and strike a match. We should establish the process. Could you say a bit about the process that you've both gone through together to get to the book.

Jacob: We voted on a set of issues that we thought would represent some of the deepest disagreements between us, and then we took each one in turn, race, gender role, homosexuality, power, morality, religion, and we first exchanged emails representing our thoughts on the matter. Then we responded to those emails, and then we responded to the response, and it ended up being phone calls until we were saturated, and felt we had really grasped something of where the other person was coming from, and really feel about the conversation, and then we moved on. And we kept notes of everything so we could go back through and piece together key moments in the exchange, and that's what the book is.

Nicholas: Great.

Phil: Well said. I was going to add that a key thing that we did, I think, is that we challenged each other with questions. We would ask each other questions, and would respond to each other's questions. So it wasn't a traditional debate, in a sense.

Jacob: Yes.

Nicholas: As I said to you by email, I'm very jealous that you've done this process, because I found it quite difficult to find someone who's a polar opposite who's willing to engage in this process, which inevitably is challenging and presses all of those emotional buttons.

Phil: Absolutely, yes.

Nicholas: It's great you've managed to do that.

Phil: It was exhausting at times, but it was very fulfilling also. Very, very worth it. Doing it in writing helped sometimes, because you could process, you could sit back and think about it, compared to confronting each other face to face, that made it a little easier. It took a lot of time.

Nicholas: Having established the framework, what I'd really like to do is throw you the hottest potato. Maybe you'd both answer it differently, Phil first, what was the topic which is the toughest, the most difficult, the most emotional triggering, the most challenging?

Phil: That's a tough one, because there's a tie, maybe, between gender roles and homosexuality. Those are the two that pushed my buttons the most, those were the two that were hardest. Maybe overall, homosexuality, gay marriage, that was a real challenge for me.

Nicholas: Great. And Jacob?

Jacob: I agree. That holds true to other conversations I've co-facilitated. My students always find that to be especially challenging.

Nicholas: The gay marriage one? Great. Well, do you mind if we roll with that, then? Who would be best to go first? If you like, lay out your original position, if you like.

Jacob: I wouldn't mind.

Nicholas: Yes.

Phil: Good.

Nicholas: By the way, what I mean to do is to find out the, if you like, the hardline original positions that you held, and then talk about the process of learning from each other, and then understand where you've come to afterwards, which of course might be the same place.

Jacob: It's never the same place for me, but it's always softer around the edges, it's always more workable. But it was also something, Nick, where I didn't convert Phil and he didn't convert me so much as a humanization, seeing nuance. I can't see Phil's views in a stereotypic sound-byte fashion anymore. I find myself telling people about leftist thought now. "Guess what I learned from this guy, because there's something that rings true to me in it."

My view on gay marriage is essentially the same view as most conservative Christians, and even members of other Judeo-Christian cultures that marriage is ordained by God, and something that He has, the decreed is between man and woman, whereas many people may say this Holy book says so, it says so in the Bible, I agree; but I would also add that for Mormons, for Latter Day Saints, our rationale for why that is, why God created man, goes back to the first book of Genesis that God created man in his own image, and for us the image of God is a man and a woman united in a relationship, that's who God is.

And for us, our spirits are literally children of God. And so we believe it's in our DNA to seek to become more like God. For Mormons, the family and marriage are not just some creation of a certain industrial period, that there really is, in our theology and our ontology, there's a sense that this view of marriage reflects our identity, and it reflects where we want to go and be, our teleology, our purpose. That's a pretty good summary.

Nicholas: And is that the polite version? Because lots of conservative Christians, or just conservatives, would say much harsher things, wouldn't they? They would say, "Homosexuality is a disease, or it's disordered, or it's evil or it's dirty. Are you putting a nice gloss on it? Really go for it.

Jacob: There's no gloss here. My dissertation chair is lesbian.

Nicholas: Yes?

Jacob: She loves her partner as much as I love my wife, she loves her daughter as much as I love my son. She's a good a human being as I am. I love her, I love my research partner who's gay, and the differences I have are not in the sense that you hear. I take issue with many things that other conservatives would say, the disgust, the pervert jokes.

Nicholas: Yes.

Jacob: But there are also other issues that I agree with. Some concerns about what does this mean for society, if it's all the same? Yes, no gloss here.

Nicholas: So regarding gay marriage, your position is what? That it shouldn't exist? We shouldn't have it?

Jacob: I want my advisor and her partner to be respected in their relationship as much as me. There's something theologically that concerns, there's something that concerns me, or if it means we have to change our theology, basically, and say marriage is something else now. I think there are other compromises that we could come to.

Nicholas: So are you saying that gay people should have the ability to have some publicly recognized union, but to call it something different, and for it to have a different legal status?

Jacob: Yes, or the same legal status as marriage with another name. I don't mind there being public recognition at all, yes.

Nicholas: Yes. And the foundation of the marriage being special is what? I didn't quite get the religious underpinning. I'm not very religious myself, so what's that got to do with becoming like God?

Jacob: Well, if God is our father and mother, we believe we left God's presence, Nick, to come to earth to have experience and learn and develop, like a child leaving home to go to college, and that the purpose of earth is kind of like college, to learn a lot, and progress and become more like our heavenly parents. So for us, family life is a caldron where that happens. We learn these lessons about loving each other, and sacrificing and serving.

Compare that with serial dating, like The Bachelor and Bachelorette. There's something about family life, including Phil's family, I don't have a problem at all saying he and his sweetheart, Eudora, they're learning some of the same kinds of lessons that my wife and I are learning. Phil's not married. But in this thing we call "family," we learn these lessons, and for us, that happens best in the context of marriage, and there's something inherent to the connection between man and woman that for us represents the ideal.

It doesn't mean that that's the only thing that I'm going to respect, or the only thing that's worthwhile. There's single-parent families, there's gay parents. I think there really is a place many conservatives need to come to where they find a level respect and love and acceptance of difference, as well.

Nicholas: Thank you. And likewise, Phil, would you mind just setting out, not the process you went through, but your original position on the subject, and why it matters to you?

Phil: Okay, I'll try. My original position was, and as a matter of fact my position still is, marriage is a legal institution and marriage is a human institution. Humans tend towards monogamy and commitment between humans, commitments of one person to another in a couple is important. Kids need to see commitment amongst the adults. So I'm a big believer in family, but for me family is not about gender, it's not about the law, it's about the love, the caring, the people involved, knowing that the other one is committed to them. That's what it's about and that's what is needed. That's what provides the safety, that's what provides the development for human beings, and for us to flourish.

So I'm maybe not like some advocates of gay marriage in that I could be fine if we just got rid of marriage entirely as a thing that the government had anything to do with, and we just went to entirely civil unions for everybody, right? And if you want to call something "marriage," that's up to you, and you and your church, if you have a church, or whatever. That's one way to deal with the problem, whereas I think a lot of gays and lesbians, they want marriage. They want that name, because the recognition isn't there for them unless they get that name, and I can understand that.

Nicholas: I see.

Phil: For me, the bottom line is homosexuality is a normal part of human populations, there's no God that ordained that deep down we're hetero-sexual, we're not more truly fulfilled in God's vision by being heterosexual or whatever. For me, none of that adds up because there isn't that theolog-ical background, that Bible instruction there, or that vision from God.

So for me, homosexuality is there, and it's not harmful. Love is love, you know? If you say that it's not the most natural thing, if you declare it, people declare it, if society, above all, declares that people are deep down really heterosexual, then homosexuals are going to be marginal-ized. They're going to be damaged. They're going to suffer from stereotypes, and they may turn away from the love and caring and commitment even as a result, right?

They need to be included in the human community, not told that they're not what they should be, which is what we're telling kids right now, and it's especially damaging, I think, for young people, when they're trying to deal with their sexual orientation that they're discovering.

Nicholas: Yes.

Phil: They get these messages that deep down, they should feel and desire the opposite sex, even if they don't.

Jacob: There's a lot, Nick, that I agree with Phil and what he just said, the piece about not marginalizing, not pressuring, not saying this is who you should be, and so pray hard enough until you're there. It's clear that that has put pressure and led to all sorts of harm. I think one interesting place that I came to with Phil in this discussion is, I also see that pressure going in the other direction. I have a friend who feels same gender attraction, but does not identify with it. He does not see it as who he is.

He has felt pressure from the gay and lesbian community that if he doesn't follow that impulse, which is one of his impulses, in a way he has an impulse as well towards heterosexuality, if he doesn't follow his homosexual impulse, then he's being untrue to himself. And so I feel like if there is space and respect for different people to follow what they feel is best and what they feel is who they are in both directions, I would be satisfied with that. But right now, there seems on both sides, and Phil would probably agree, is pressure, this is who you are. This is who you are. No, this is who you are!

Nicholas: Yes.

Jacob: And perhaps just agreeing that we disagree on identity, and that's okay. And let's agree that it's okay to disagree. I disagree with Phil on identity. I believe I'm a child of God and I believe Phil is, and he doesn't.

Nicholas: Yes.

Jacob: And that's okay.

Nicholas: I don't want to stir up an argument just for entertainment value, but obviously you guys are good friends, and you've talked about this stuff for a long time. You've both come across as really friendly, very reasonable people who are putting across a reasonable position. And having listened to what you've both said, I personally didn't get kind of moved or triggered in any way, and I didn't feel that real polarity between you. I didn't feel like if you were in the same room, you'd be about to strangle each other.

So I've missed why this is such a live issue. What is it that's really pressed your buttons and made you angry, and why was this a subject which was so difficult for you to come together on?

Phil: We are friends, and we are friendly. But I think there is deep disagreement, and a difficulty is the way we move in conversation, Jacob, you and I, away from a disagreement towards these other things that I love moving towards, where we find that overlap where we can appreciate each other. There's a shift that goes on, and I don't know how to put it into words, sometimes. I'll try this.

Jacob, you say and believe that there's a pressure in both directions, and that we should accept people and not pressure them as principle, and yet you endorse the view that deep down, we're all heterosexual, right? That that's God's plan, that's there in scripture, that's how we were before we came to be humans on this earth, in this life, at "college," so to speak, that of the things that we're going to learn is that we're really heterosexual, right? So it seems to me you are sending the message that you say we shouldn't send. And so that frustrates me. Or it's frustrating as soon as we move away from that towards the parts where we agree.

Also, I don't see the pressure as equal, in any way, shape or form. It's true that there are those communities, those places where people will feel pressure from the gay or lesbian community to live their true gay identity, if they reveal that they have some feelings in that direction, and that's identity politics, which I have a problem with.

Nicholas: Why do you care about that though, Phil? That's kind of an interesting intellectual position, but so what? Why does it matter? Why does it matter to you?

Phil: Why does it matter to me if people pressure other people?

Nicholas: Just this subject of gay marriage, for and against? Why-

Phil: Well, I've seen vicious prejudice, I see my gay and lesbian friends afraid, physically afraid for their lives in context. I see them not be able to free be in this planet. My friends Michael and Mark, they can't walk down the street holding hands safely in Potsdam, New York. I mean, maybe they could and they'd be fine. It's a big risk for them to take, just to walk down the street holding hands. They're a couple.

Nicholas: And why-

Phil: That to me is a problem.

Nicholas: What's the difficulty with the conservative position on the subject?

Phil: Well, there are different conservative positions that I am so appreciative, Jacob, that you are not saying things like, "Homosexuality is dirty, it's disgusting, these people are perverted." So there are different conservative positions. It seems to me that all of them say that really, deep down, those people are not who they really are, or are somehow wrong for society for them to act out and fully be what they feel.

I don't think what they feel is harmful or bad. I don't think we should all act out on everything we feel. That's a myth about liberals, I think, or leftists, that we're just for every feeling being expressed, no matter what it is, people do have some bad feelings and pleasures they shouldn't honor, desires they shouldn't honor. But homosexuality is just sexuality, you know?

Nicholas: Right. And Jacob, likewise, you spoke in a very reasoned, generous and sensitive way. I haven't quite understood what's the big deal for you? If you said this was the subject you most conflicted over, what was it that got under your skin, or that you really disapprove of in the liberal or leftist position on gay marriage?

Jacob: Well, the issue that really got under our skin the most was writing together. That was the hardest, being co-authors! To be clear, Nick, I say this is the most sensitive issue because others struggle with it.

Nicholas: Oh, okay.

Jacob: I've seen families torn apart. I've seen people walk away from this church I am involved in after years just because of this issue. It strikes at identity. I don't personally-

Nicholas: I see. Yes, I get it.

Jacob: I find there's a frame, that if you understand that frame, you can have a conversation like me and Phil, and you can say, "Hey, I can love you." I was really transformed during graduate school by my friends in the gay and lesbian community. So I'm excited to help others have this kind of conversation so it's not so deeply painful.

And let me just respond to Phil's earlier question. It's true, I do hold a more absolute view than the gay and lesbian community about the nature of this. I think the difference, Phil, is, I'm willing to not go out and pressure everyone who's gay and try to convince them that this is who they have to be, and who they should be, and the pervert jokes. And your comment about your friends not walking down the street makes me sad, too. I feel like I can hold that position and have conviction on it and not cross that line.

So there's a difference there, in terms of you can be strong in a view without making someone else uncomfortable. I can believe that marriage is really valuable in how two people should live together, but ask Phil if he's ever been uncomfortable with what he calls "living in sin." I've never called it that.

Nicholas: Right.

Phil: To me, this issue connects to our gender roles chapter, because in the gender roles chapter, Jacob, you argue that we should teach boys and girls that when they grow up to be men and women, that there are duties that go with each gender, or emphases appropriate for each gender. To me, if we teach that in our institutions, it is pressure. If we teach that marriage is a man and a woman, one's a nurturer, one's a protector-provider, and if we teach that, there's pressure. It's well and good for you to say, "Let's not pressure, I won't pressure," you see what I'm saying?

Jacob: Yes. I would come back and say it depends on where we teach it. I'm going to teach that to William, I'll teach it in my Sunday School class, but when we get into a setting where it is public schools and in the public square, what do we do?

Nicholas: Right.

Jacob: My view, in the public square, we do this kind of conversation. If there are church members and families and communities where this is taught, others where the opposite is taught, people can find communities, what they're drawn to. But both have a right to teach it, if that makes sense. To teach their respective views.

Nicholas: Thanks guys. Obviously, you've been demonstrating your discussion and the process there. Having thrashed out that subject in depth, what changed? Did you come to respect one another's positions, or did you even change your own position and find a more transpartisan position?

Jacob: I would describe my change as just a softening around the edges that, I understand fills you as nuanced and reasonable and human, and all the things that I think get lost in the echo chamber where Phil's a liberal atheist secular guy that is against religion and against marriage and against fatherhood. I can't stomach that kind of rhetoric from conservative self-proclaimed spokespersons, because I know Phil, and because I know others like him.

I frequently say something like this to a friend of mine that hates Obama. I say, "I know how you feel. I also have concerns about some of Obama's choices. But let me say, I know a lot of people like Obama. I know them really well. And every one of them really believes that this is the better way to go, and they're not trying to destroy America. So I reference my relationship other conservatives understand. You can disagree vociferously with someone and not despise them and not question their motives and not claim they're a demon, you know what I mean?

Nicholas: So you respect the position more. Is there anything that Phil persuaded you about, or is there anything that you've now incorporated, added to your own view?

Jacob: A lot. A lot. If I could depart from this issue and tell you one thing that I have talked about frequently since my discussion with Phil, is some of the core tenets of leftists' thoughts wherein a system takes on a life of its own, and people within the system kind of get swept away, I did my dissertation on antidepressants and Prozac, and I have found some of Phil's analyses to be right on. And this word that was scary to me, and was scary and that's a liberal thing, I reference it now with conservatives as we talk about the role of big business and being in business who had a hand in writing some of this latest healthcare legislation. It's really opened my eyes to hear some of Phil's thoughts.

So there are a lot of other examples on a smaller level. Phil, do you want to comment?

Phil: Well, getting back to the gay issue, homosexuality issue, maybe this was the chapter where we found the least common ground, right, and yet even in this chapter, even in that conversation, after the conversation was over between you and me, I see more possibility for some kind of transpartisan agreement, despite the disagreements. It's not that you and I agree more than before, it's not that you persuaded me on the gay marriage issue to change, so I can't say that that happened.

It's not just mutual respect, Nick, it's mutual understanding. That can be a building block for something. And in this case, it could be a building block for example for civil unions. I mean, imagine if many conservatives who oppose gay marriage came out strongly for civil unions, instead of against it, and imagine if many gays and lesbians said, you know, on the gay marriage part of the equation, we need to be more accepting or give more time, because I understand how much that's a bottom line for those other people. That for them, marriage is sacred, and it's defined a certain that's sacred, and it's not simply a matter of rights, everyone having the right to get married.

We, the gay and lesbian community, are asking them, the conservatives, to change their view of marriage, and that's asking a lot. So maybe there would be some accommodation that could happen because of mutual understanding. It was exciting to have the conversation with Jacob, because I could see, this could happen. If people talked enough across these boundaries, that could happen, despite, yes, we'd still intensely disagree.

Nicholas: Listening to you speak there, Phil, I was thinking, well, I suppose the underlying assumption that in order to live together within a country or a civilization or a community or whatever, we have to agree so that one bunch has to agree with the other bunch, and we have to some shared rules and so on. But of course, looked at in complexity, or in kind of pluralism, you could say it's completely possible for all kinds of different people with different views to live together simultaneously kind of in paradox. And some people might harden that into the multicultural ideology of which itself comes in lots of different strands. But it could also just put it down to a common sense of complexity.

Phil: Yes. Well, one expression of multiculturalism is, all cultures are equally good because it's your culture, and lets them all live together. I say instead let's encounter each other, and challenge each other, and live together in a community of disagreement where we engage each other. And I think not only is that okay or possible, but actually, it's better than agreement.

If you look at any organization where there's disagreement flourishing in the organization and people listen and talk to each other, you'll see they outperform the organizations where there isn't the disagreement, right? Because disagreement corrects error. Disagreement pushes people to clarify their positions. Actually, let's take our ideal community. We want community. And let's think of a great community, a perfect community as one where there is disagreement. How about that?

Nicholas: Yes. Now this might not be so relevant to you, and maybe more of a European thing, but I was interested to ask about your opinions on immigration in general, and specifically, because of the religious angle, Islamic immigration. Because into Europe, historically, we had, other than the mediaeval attempts to colonize Spain, the Balkans and Sicily, there were no Muslims significantly in Europe.

Phil: Right.

Nicholas: Really, since the second World War, particularly since the 60s, 70s, 80s and beyond, there's been a huge influx. In Britain, it's mixed up with all sorts of other people. But in many European countries like France, Holland, Sweden, Germany, their immigrants, like yours are Hispanic, ours predominantly are Muslim. Obviously, that's not happening in a vacuum, it's happening at a time when we have multiculturalism as an ideology, and largely in the first form you describe of patronizing people, patting them on the head and it's actually rather racist, telling them that they can never be a member and they're separate, and they're a victim group that need special protection. We've had relativism and self-loathing. Imagine in Holland, we've got a very postmodern liberal educated mostly secular post-Christian society in which they pride themselves on being tolerant and open and sensitive, and then of course you can't caricature the Islamic population, because they'll come from lots of different strata, backgrounds and levels of development, and so on.

But there, the average weight of the culture is much more at the traditional level, the traditional, conservative, patriarchal, absolutistic. And generally speaking, when one meets the other, the one, I'd imagine that the sensitive liberal pluralist self-loathing relativist would surrender, and the one with the more aggressive views who's willing to fight and die would win. Have you thought about that? How do we live with that challenge?

Jacob: Nick, I love what Phil just finished saying about a disagreement-welcoming society. It's fair to say that conservatives, well, all communities struggle with that. All communities that have conviction and ideology, conservative and liberal. In a way, Mormons and other Christians agree a lot with Islam and Muslims. In fact, at the United Nations, when the traditional family issues have come up, Muslim and Mormon and Catholic, it's been a religious coalition that has come at odds with the feminists, liberal, secular coalition.

Nicholas: Yes.

Jacob: What I would say is the same flowering and opening that I am excited about seeing continue to happen within my own conservative community I hope continues within the Islamic community. Namely, I had graduate student friends who are Muslim, and they were thinking for themselves, and students asking lovely questions, exploring courses of critical inquiry, and with the Arab Spring, I feel like there is a new sense that Islam is not incompatible with free thinking, and thinking for themselves.

Can they be participants in this disagreement society? I think so. I think it will be harder for some reasons in their theology, but we're seeing some exciting things happen.

Nicholas: There's no question that that's true, say, amongst more educated, more sophisticated people living in relatively affluent, pleasant places, at University and so on.

But what would you say to those Europeans who live in poorer districts, or rougher districts, where actually they're having people physically force them on the street to change their behavior and imposing their way of life, people acting in a very foreign way, dressing differently, bringing in a different culture, and that feels to some like colonization? How would you recommend that the sensitive, pluralistic, liberal Dutch or Swedes or French are open to diversity, but without being colonized and dominated?

Jacob: Well, correct me if I'm wrong, I want to hear Phil, but Phil, when you say you want a society that where disagreement is respected and embraced, there are also core things that we agree on, right? I mean, for instance, this issue of, should we force someone to follow a belief system looking to Christian history or looking forward to the fears of some Islamic pressure? I think we can agree as a society on some things like that, but it's not okay to beat up your family. It's not okay to impose and force and coerce conversion.

I think Islamic democracies are wrestling with this right now and will continue to. But there are some things we have to agree on, or else we're not a community. I think there are some core things. I'm a community psychologist, Nick, and at the heart of a community are also some shared understandings alongside the disagreements. If everything, if all the shared agreements go away, we might be in a tough spot.

Phil: Yes. A couple of things right away, first of all, being a pro-disagreement society doesn't mean people disagree about everything, right? You engage disagreement, and you discover agreement along with disagreement, right? Also, there's a paradox, if you like, but it's there. I'm taking the position that disagreement is good, that's a position. So it's not neutral. That is to say, those who want to impose a way of life on other people, rather than talk about it and argue for their way of life, right, and engage in disagreement, I'm saying to them, you have to change, right? So I'm not open to every position equally. The position that's anti-disagreement I am not open to as equally as the position that's pro-disagreement.

However, I recognize even that position as one worth hearing, right? So I say to a person who wants to tell me how to dress or how to live, and exactly how to conduct myself in all my affairs in public and private, I want to hear more and I want to learn why you feel this way, and what's so important about it to you, and I'm willing to listen. However, I insist that you accord me the same treatment, and that we learn together in a public square where we can disagree about those things. That is a challenge to fundamentalism of any kind.

In every religious tradition, major religious tradition, there are pro-disagreement elements. There are also fundamentalist dangers lurking, if I can use that word, "fundamentalism." And yes, right now I think Islam faces the challenge of sticking to Islam, Muslim people sticking to being Muslim, and yet being pro-disagreement, and therefore living with others and listening to them as people they respect. Maybe I can more freely say that, or maybe it's in a way add more credibility saying that because I'm not Christian, I'm not Jewish, right? So I'm not looking for some other religion telling them to change their religion. I don't have a religion. I'm saying, yes, each major religion needs a revolution towards their pro-disagreement elements, right? That's, I guess, my position.

Nicholas: So Phil, I can't disagree with that, that sounds great. And the majority, we'd probably run with you on that, because they are just people getting on with their lives, and not particularly energized, but there will be some who will want to push you. Push, and radically disagree with you. How do sensitive pluralistic open tolerant liberal democrats assert themselves? In other words, what's a healthy boundary? How far do you have to be pushed before you say, "No?" How much can you accommodate? Where's the boundary on this?

Phil: Peaceful, no coercion. The coercion is only about the rules necessary to live together, right? At the regulations that we need. So we have coercion, you've got to pay taxes because together we need a system that spends some money on cleaning up the environment and providing education and infrastructure. Yes, we need some coercion, but we need some prisons maybe, unfortunately, and so on. But coercion is not otherwise acceptable, right? And so, that's that, right?

And then, isn't that very clear? Why is that such a hard line? Yes, I'm sensitive, but that doesn't mean that if someone punches me in the face I'm going to say, "Oh, please punch me again, because that's your belief."

Nicholas: Yes.

Phil: Right?

Nicholas: Yes. Well, perhaps it's more of a European thing. I recently, in Britain at the moment, there are a whole series of court cases going on around the country of gangs of pedophiles from Muslim backgrounds who have been raping young white girls. It's something that's been known for a long time, on the street level, people have known that that's been an issue.

But insanely, in spite of the fact we're meant to live under the rule of law and democracy, the rights of those girls has not been looked after. Until very recently, the police and the authorities have not tackled that. And the reason they haven't tackled it is because they're desperately afraid of being called "racist," and desperately afraid of being called "Islamophobic," and they'd rather allow girls, young vulnerable white girls to be raped than to do their job, because they're so scared of putting down a healthy boundary, that's how sick our culture is. That's an extreme example, but there are many more.

Phil: Oh! There are. Female genital mutilation I think is wrong, and it's not right just because it's in someone's culture. It's wrong in my opinion, and it's a practice that ought not be legal. I understand why people are reluctant to follow the law and apply it, but they should, right? Jacob, what do you think?

Jacob: Well, you're talking about a hesitancy, Nick, to step in and say, "This is not okay, and I'm going to draw a line." And as a member of a community that does that willingly, I was a missionary in Brazil for two years knocking on doors, sharing truth. I've noticed that people are really hesitant to share where they're coming from, because they don't want to offend.

Nicholas: Yes.

Jacob: It's almost like, "Thou shalt not offend," is the first commandment, kind of taking over. We don't want to step on anyone's toes. I want to say, what happened to sharing goodness, truth that you have? When it gets to the point that innocent people are not being protected, or we're losing the healthy accountability of communities, I just think maybe it's an issue of being too worried about offending. And that's where Phil's point about a disagreement society is crucial. If we see something that doesn't sit well, let's have freedom to bring it out and let's have a public square where that is happening.

And this whole Penn State trial where someone is held accountable and will revolt it at the sexual abuse and the domestic violence, and that's a shared universal understanding, rather than something we wink at. I think we're moving in that direction. I published a paper on domestic violence and community accountability, and there's a real need for accountability. And I think it goes back to what Phil said.

Nicholas: Yes. So when you see a postmodern relativistic sensitive pluralistic liberal desperately trying not to offend, and being really trying hard to see things from the others' perspective and accommodating many different ways of being, how do you see that through a conservative lens? Are they just foolish, or directionless?

Jacob: No, they're not. They're trying to be sensitive and kind. I don't have a problem with that at all. I get along more with my liberal friends than I do with my conservative friends, because they're trying to do that. I think it's a wonderful thing for the community. All I would say is, let's just agree that we all have conviction.

Nicholas: Yes.

Jacob: And it's impossible to be truly relativistic, even the position of relativism is a conviction that relativism is reality.

Nicholas: Obviously the Mormons have been in America from a very early stage. And could be that there are lessons from the way that Mormons live in America, and manage to live alongside a huge diversity of different culture, but still get along, still obey the law, still thrive and are successful, and are still patriotic Americans, rather than being kind of a foreign enemy, or a problem? Are there lessons about, for the Muslim community in Europe of how to make that a success without conflict?

Jacob: We have been hurt by persecution in the past, and we know how it feels to be persecuted and driven for our beliefs. No community should feel that, not the gay and lesbian community, not the liberal secular. We ought to be able to get to a place where we can have a larger community and respect it. When Mormons were driven to Utah, they came to accept the authority of the government. We do believe in obeying the law and authority.

Nicholas: As a truly religious person, you must believe that all the laws and the way we live, the choices we make should be God's, or religious-derived. You have to live in a country where a very large proportion are like Phil, and simply don't believe that. And also, others who come from different religions. How do you make that work without having to fight, or be in conflict?

Phil: Jacob, I have an idea that might prompt you, the swimming pool incident. You could tell about that. You handled that without trying to force people on the issue, right?

Jacob: Yes. We had a pool built in our local community, Nick. The majority of the population here is religious, and Christian and following the Sabbath on Sunday. And so, when it came to the issue of whether the pool was closed on Sunday, there was a big, divisive conversation of both sides trying to force their way, that we wanted the pool to be closed on Sunday. We want it to be open. And you're imposing your values on us, and so on. I'm not denying that there are tricky compromises that have to be worked out, I think I would just say everything will be easier, and the compromises will be easier if we are open to the humanity of those who are disagreeing with us.

That you can want to go to the pool on Sunday and still be someone worth listening to, and I can try to work out something that works for you, too. And that conversation just isn't happening very much. Look at the American Congress right now. We get in our positions and focus all our energies on just making sure we get our way, like kids in a sandbox, is an analogy that Phil and I use. I'm just curious to see what could happen if this manner of conversation were to become more predominant. It's certainly not something I see very often. It's kind of an endangered species, of sorts, when it comes to conversation.

Nicholas: What are the lessons for broader American and Western culture, or global culture, regarding politics, dialogue, community from your book? What are the lessons that we should all take on board?

Phil: One lesson connects to what you said just a few moments ago, Nick. The lesson is, we can combine disagreement with a belief in truth, okay? Postmodernism has taught me many things, postmodernist theory. To claim that there is no truth because of the construction is problematic, however, or it can be misunderstood. The things I believe are true I recognize can be argued with. That is to say, I can't prove they're true, but I still believe them. I still believe them, I still believe that there is truth.

I believe you can have a society where we engage in disagreement strongly, because A, we think of something worth listening to on the other side, and B, we're not relativists. We think there's truth to be discovered if we talk. It's not about simply accepting the other point of view, meaning you don't agree, you just let it be. No. You challenge it, but you listen to it. And that can work. But it's a fine line. And that could help your sensitive liberal friends who don't want to offend anyone.

Nicholas: Yes. Jacob, what were the lessons from your book?

Jacob: Beautiful. I would add that there's a safety in what Phil's talking about. I've been alarmed at the power of big institutions, whether we're talking about big business, big government, big religion, big media, big pharma. These institutions to shape the conversation so that we're no longer talking as one citizen to another, informed about things as they are, but we are downloading narratives that have been manufactured by the very powerful industries that serve an interest other than our human welfare. So there's the leftist inside of Phil coming across.

This conversation is happening in a larger system that is troubled, and maybe if we can do what Phil's talking about well and broadly, maybe that can be some kind of a check on these larger institutions, where the power of the larger institution, whether religious, business, that is held in check by a people that says, look, we're thinking still, we're asking questions and we're talking across the differences. And what you're saying, Bill O'Reilly, or what you're saying ... What these people are saying is not ringing true to normal human beings, and holding our institutions accountable so we're not so manipulated and driven by them.

Phil: Beautiful.

Nicholas: It's easy to see, just as we're doing now, amongst friendly, well-motivated people who want to engage with a dialogue or a transpartisan process. But it's a much different thing to scale that up to the level of a nation, or beyond. How could we institutionalize that in our political process, and our media process, so as to get from the current tribal partisan fighting to a transpartisan position that draws the healthy, positive strand out of all the different dimensions?

Jacob: Beautiful question! I'd love to hear what Phil has to say.

Phil: Thank you. There are techniques people can utilize to have these kind of conversations with each other, even before they're friends, or without being friends. And they can start trying to do that on the micro level by taking advantage of those techniques. There's a little bravery, a little jumping in required, but it can happen. And that's a micro kind of movement that can change what happens at the macro level.

Then, there are things you can do at the macro level as well. So at a micro level, I'd say to people, Google or search for "study circles." Learn about "study circles," the concept of these circles where people ... That's the right term, right, Jacob?

Jacob: Yes.

Phil: Where people of disagreeing points of view meet in groups of four or five to share views and give each other equal time, and get to know one another in a kind of public space, without trying to make a decision together.

Then there are macro things. Citizen juries that take place in different countries, where a randomly selected group of citizens are meant to represent the diverse parts of the community meet and talk about an issue not for a day, but maybe for a week.

Nicholas: Yes.

Phil: And they get some financial support to do so, and they bring in experts and ask them questions. And then they make a series of recommendations to their legislators, so that it's not just people voting on what they want. They're learning something, and then they're speaking together about what they could agree on. And that speaks powerfully to the legislatures. It brings an element of dialogue into decision-making at the political level. So there are many things going on that could be done at once to change the culture.

Jacob: That was beautiful! I like what you said. I think the kind of thing you're doing, Nick, is facilitating that, and anybody that speaks up.

Nicholas: So if we go right to the sort of very biggest picture, if everyone engaged in this sort of process that you've done across their lives, at home, at work, in politics, and integrated the healthy positive strands of all, left and right, male and female, et cetera, et cetera, what kind of a world would it be? How would it be different?

Phil: Wow.

Nicholas: What's the potential that we unleash?

Phil: It would be very different. Obviously, it's a tall order, right? People are so busy, for one thing, it takes a certain amount of time. So not everyone has to participate at the same level, the same amount of intensity, I don't want to give that impression, because that would just make some people say, "I can't do that." But I think a diffusing of tension. I think many times, win-win solutions to public problems, even amongst people who disagree.

So, for example, Jacob and I discovered, you know, we have some common ground on domestic violence and opposing domestic violence, with different narratives behind it about gender and so forth, but nonetheless, we both consider it a major problem. Gratuitous sex and violence in the media. A lot of conservatives are upset about that, liberals are upset about that in different ways. So we could have a world where what we see in the media is different and more healthy, and yet we don't have censorship, just to give you an example.

Jacob: Beautiful! My mentor, Julian Rappaport is one of the fathers of community psychology. He liked to say that communities have a power in them that we haven't figured out how to tap. It's kind of nuclear power. We have to figure out how to get to it. And he said that as we learn better ways to nurture the innate the capacity of communities, we can see a new kind of power unleashed. I believe that. Religiously speaking, I do believe in Zion.

I believe some of the dilemmas that do seem to be intractable dilemmas right now could be resolved. We could get to a society where there are no poor among us, that's a verse from our scripture. And that's what Zion is for us. It's a society where all tears are wiped away. And you're not shot for protesting in the streets in Syria. Where humanity is taking care of itself. I think we can go somewhere. I think none of us have a clear view of what that beautiful society looks like, but it seems like people from different perspectives, including Phil, we see that there's potential we can move towards together. And that's exciting.

Nicholas: That's fantastic! The last question, where are you both going with this next? Is the book the end of the line, or are you taking this further?

Jacob: We'll be presenting that at the National Coalition of Dialogue and Liberation, actually facilitating the workshop in Seattle. I wish you could make it, Nick. But our secret plot is, we're getting together with other leaders at this conference of liberal conservative dialogue, where other people interested in the transpartisan conversation, and we're going to create an app, and it's going to be free, and we're going to be circulate it and hopefully make it good enough that it goes viral.

Nicholas: Wow!

Jacob: There's a lot of stupid things that go viral on the Internet, maybe something nice and helpful can! We can include your Web site. It's this idea of let's put it in the palm of people's hands. So if you're tired of this, well, then there's an option.

Nicholas: Yes.

Phil: Yes. I think we, in the future we go forward trying to spread the message and work with others to spread the message, and help others do the kind of thing we did, but in their own way. That's what we have to do going forward. I don't know that we'll write together again in the short term, we both need a rest from co-authoring. But we definitely want to keep it up, maybe do workshops. I envision we could do some kind of performance thing at high schools or something, where we visit and we, together, Jacob, and we act out one of our disagreements. And at the end, we disagree still, but we show our mutual understanding. That kind of thing. Or other people could do that. Through drama. They would mime, they would mimic this, they would display this kind of disagreement.

Nicholas: So finally, if someone would like to get in touch with you and to, or to buy your book, or to connect with your work, what's the best way to do that?

Phil: They can Google et cetera to find my e-mail address and they can e-mail me, and they can call me at SUNY Potsdam, State University of New York College at Potsdam. We have a Facebook site for the book, *You're Not as Crazy as I Thought*, which his easy to find on Facebook. Amazon.com, Barnes and Noble, et cetera, they carry the book. Potomac Books is the publisher. You can go to their catalog online, so there are many ways online to buy the book. A good thing is maybe go to a bookstore and ask them to order the book, so maybe they'll find out about the book. So if someone wants to promote the book, that's a nice thing to do.

Nicholas: Thank you.

Phil: We created a blog space. Not many people go to it yet, but we've posted a few excerpts from the book there, and a few people go there to learn about it, it's Political-Dialogue.com.

Nicholas: So, thanks so much, I really enjoyed talking to you both. Great fun, and it's lovely to see the depth to which you've taken this!

Phil: Oh my goodness, thank you so much! It's just been awesome.

Jacob: Thank you, Nick.

Phil: Great, Nick.

Jacob: You're a delightful soul, Nick, when you come to Utah, let me know, so I can take care of you, alright?

Nicholas: I'd like to very much, thank you!

Jacob: A ski trip. Thanks, guys!

Phil: Bye, Jacob.

Nicholas: Thank you very much, indeed!

The Future of Western Civilization

Progress Report

Melanie Mortiboys interviews Dr Nicholas Beecroft
Melanie Mortiboys interviews Dr Nicholas Beecroft for this Progress Report on the project exploring the Future of Western Civilization in the light of the interviews so far.

Melanie Mortiboys is a writer, artist, Pilates teacher, Bowen therapist, mother and Nicholas' girlfriend. She has been a key catalyst of the Future of Western Civilization behind the scenes, offering her wisdom, support, encouragement and judgement throughout. She studied Drama, Film and Television at Bristol University and has since explored the world of personal development, psychology and health. She is currently working on her first novel.

Melanie: Hello Nicholas.

Nicholas: Hello, Melanie.

Melanie: So it's a really exciting day today because I've been given the opportunity to put you on your casting couch. (laughs) So hello and welcome. Today it's my turn, Melanie Mortiboys to interview Dr. Nicholas Beecroft, Consultant Psychiatrist exploring the Future of Western Civilization through a series of interviews with visionary leaders. It was some 6 months ago that I first interviewed Nicholas at the start of this project when he was saying what his mission was and what he wanted to with the project, and now it's time to take stock and evaluate what's happened and put Nicholas in the chair too, I think. So, Nicholas.

Nicholas: Hello, Melanie.

Melanie: Lovely to turn the tables and it's a really exciting opportunity for me to ask you some important questions that maybe the readers of your interviews would also like to ask. How do you feel, after this amount of time, where you are right now and what you've achieved?

Nicholas: Well, it's been an incredibly exciting project, really interesting. I got off to a slow start at the beginning of 2011 but really got going in September 2011. I kicked into action by going down to St. Paul's Cathedral to interview the people at the Occupy protest. Really, since then, it's taken on a momentum of its own, and well, I've had a great time really, had lots of fun, met lots of very, very interesting people, and lots more ahead.

Melanie: Well, yes, it is very, very exciting. I'd like to backtrack slightly and ask what's your purpose behind it? Why did you start such a mission that for some might seem impossible, because to analyze the future of Western Civilization and then trying to inspire hope and show people what's on offer rather than just watching the news at 10 o'clock and see all the pain and the misery and feel, "I can't do anything. I don't know how to cope," you're offering opportunity, wisdom, insight, humor, different angles that some may or may not agree with.

Nicholas: Well, you've answered the question for me by the sound of it! Rewind to my childhood; growing up in the period of the 70s and 80s, it was a very depressing time, really, a time I perceived as a time of decay, everything falling apart, old structures, and I could feel it viscerally around me, and I really didn't like that. I think, as you rightly say, if we listen to the news, if you listen to the radio or read the newspaper, we're bombarded with negativity.

There's a huge long list of potential disasters and terrible things that may happen and are happening and so on, and that all feels really heavy and weighty, and I think really I suppose I've been on a journey to try and work out a positive way forwards. It's as simple as that really. A few years ago I realized that it isn't as bad as the media are making out. The media naturally goes for negative information, negative threat-based information, because we're designed to be alert to that; sex, food, and threats are pretty important stimuli.

However, some of these negative things are true, but to look from a different angle, actually, we are in the most amazing time. All of the things about modernity, the growth of science, the growth in our culture, the growth in human potential, it's just going faster and faster and faster. More technology, more ideas. People all over the world are experimenting with different ways of doing things, new initiatives, and sure, there are those problems, but really, the pace of human learning and the pace of change because of the internet, because of travel, because of the way that we're able to communicate now, is infinitely faster, so just as the threats are huge, the opportunities are vast.

The aim of the project was to begin to connect with many of those visionary leaders and entrepreneurs who are doing exciting things, new initiatives, or people who can really tell the positive story of who we are and where we're going. The aim was to draw them together and give them a platform to share those stories and also to dig down and test them out a bit, to see how practical they are, to see where they're working, really as a resource to share, to inspire people, and as you say, to bring hope to those who are feeling hopeless and negative, and yes, to play my role in our global conscious evolution.

Melanie: Who do you find your main followers amongst viewers at the videos?

Nicholas: Well, 32,000 people have watched them on YouTube. Roughly, the same amount have listened on iTunes or other downloads or direct on the website. The statistics are that, I suppose, about 55% are male, 45% female. The majority are between 25 and 65, so I suppose the majority of the population, but weighted probably from about 30 to 65 is the biggest group, particularly in the English-speaking countries, America, Britain, Australia, Canada, India, Singapore, New Zealand, and also closely aligned countries within Europe, Germany, Holland, Sweden, and so on, and really a scattering of people elsewhere. There have also been a lot of communications with people from non-Western countries, interested to put across their views.

From the people that I directly have contact with, lots of people who resonate with that way of thinking, so a combination of people who are visionary leaders and doing innovative evolutionary type work, and also people who have been feeling a lot of frustration and hopelessness and are interested to listen to people who've got a positive way forward.

Melanie: How do you foresee it going further now? What are your dreams for your own project?

Nicholas: There are many more subjects that I'd like to cover. I'm going to be talking to some people about masculinity, femininity, and how they relate to community. I'm going to be talking to a lady who uses music to really inspire and integrate people. I'd like to find someone who can talk about authority and the way that that is evolving, about the way that our cultural boundaries operate, what is a healthy boundary.

I've got a really great speaker coming up, a lady from Birmingham who's done some really interesting work on inspiring black people to integrate and to really get involved in the democratic process. I would really like to find someone who can talk about energy security as well as energy sustainability, because both of those tend to be separate, and my feeling is they should come together.

I've got a great Tantric speaker on love and sex, and there's going to be a speaker coming up on integrating sexual diversity into the way that we live. Someone's going to be talking about parenting and the sort of healthy inspiration and human potential and boundaries in that context.

Melanie: Fantastic. That's is really, really exciting. I was asking, so I kind of know through the pipeline that you are writing a book, and I'm just curious to know a bit more about that.

Nicholas: I see. Yes. Well, in a way I chose this format because partly as a psychiatrist but also just as a person generally, I seem to get my most creative space, my best thinking space and creative space, in relation to others, particularly in a dialogue, so this is my natural, most easy format, really, but yes, there's a job going on in the background to really integrate and synthesize the lessons and the observations from this project.

The book is to integrate the lessons coming from these interviews, but also grounded in the work that I've done over the years. My aim for that is that that will be a book which will … it's pretty insanely mega-lomaniac in its breadth, but the aim is to put Western Civilization on the psychiatrist's couch.

Melanie: Mmm.

Nicholas: Similar to what I did for the British-Syrian relationship, for example, or the War on Terror. The aim is to ask, who are we, where are we going, what's our identity, and what's the vision and the values and the future around which we're aligning ourselves? What are the wounds that need healing? Where is that energy flowing? The boundaries, the truth and falsehood, the conflicts and so on, and of course, then to make some suggestions as to where we're headed. No one person has all the answers, absolutely not, but of course, I will have my own opinion and give some suggestions as ways forward in terms of principles or vision and so on.

Melanie: Exciting.

Nicholas: Then, the aim will be to really share that and, I suppose, go around and speak about that, and my intention will be to have some group processes where people come to listen but also to participate; focused on groups, on companies, on political associations and members of the public, to really help draw them in as to what is their role in the big picture? What is the big picture? What's the map to align and calibrate their compass and to align their own mission and energy with their place in that?

Melanie: Fantastic. How exciting. So what has been your biggest lesson so far from your project?

Nicholas: I think the biggest picture one is that I feel a lot more optimistic than I did when I started. I've met both directly in the interviews but also all the people who've contacted me privately a lot of very positive people doing amazing work, and those are not unrealistic, naïve people who live in la-la-land and are not connected to see the problems that there are in the world, but they're people who see those but can see a way forward, and that's given me a huge optimism really.

I think things, in spite of all the many disaster scenarios that could occur, I think things are going to be okay and much better than okay actually. I think we can have a lot of optimism for the future notwithstanding the huge risks that might happen if we don't sort ourselves out.

Melanie: What have been your main highlights so far?

Nicholas: The interview with Neil Howe on generations I found particularly insightful. It helped me place myself in the map in a way that I hadn't done before. He's done some very interesting work on looking at the cycling of generations not just within our own lifetime but going back 500 years and spotting the patterns, and that is fascinating. I instantly could see how I slotted into the generation he calls it the Nomad generation who were born in the 70s when the previous generation, the baby boomer generation had torn everything up, torn up all the rule books and were pulling all the structures down, which had been created in turn by the Hero generation of the Second World War.

The way he described it and seeing the historical perspective of that made me feel less alone. That's the way it was, and ... but also very positively seeing the way forward, so actually were now going into an incredible, as he calls it, our fourth turning, but a real phase of transition where everything is up in the air, all the rules are up in the air, and the world will be remade by a new emerging Hero generation, and the job of us who a bit older is to help steward that process.

That was one highlight. I mean, too many others to mention really. The work of Don Beck in Spiral Dynamics runs throughout the series. He's a great visionary and someone who likewise has done incredible work in showing the cultural evolution that we're going through and how we sit in that, and again, having a framework that lets us get beyond worrying about the negative stuff and seeing the journey that we're on.

Actually another highlight most certainly was with a chap called Martin Rutte, who ...

Melanie: Heaven On Earth?

Nicholas: Yes, Project Heaven On Earth, and at first I cringed at that terminology, because not being religious it sounds creepy and religious, and in Britain, as Tony Blair said, we don't do religion, but actually what he's getting at is the huge power and unleashing of potential that comes from asking ourselves the question, not what are all the things you hate and don't like and what are all the problems and what are all the challenges, but what kind of world would you like in the best Heaven on Earth. What is the best possible outcome?

I resonated with that because I'd found that in my own experience that I'd spent an awful lot of energy to fighting things that I didn't like, like political correctness or multiculturalism or the machine model of management and so on, and of course, that just makes those forces fight back much harder and become more powerful.

Melanie: So let me interrupt there and ask you what would your Heaven on Earth be, Nicholas? It's an appropriate time to ask.

Nicholas: (laughs) I've got to walk my talk. Top line, the maximization of human potential, which sounds a bit theoretical but that really means that me, you, everyone around us, everyone on earth, we act and live in a way and create structures, whether it be education, health, military, etc., to create the best platform for us all to be the best and unfold, blossom in our lives as much as we can be, whether as teachers, as parents, as nurses, and entrepreneurs, and so on.

A world like that. A world of freedom, a world of opportunity, which is safe, secure, and with lots of love. Not a naïve world. A world that has strong boundaries. A world that has safe boundaries and security as well with discipline, authority, and so on.

Melanie: So why do you think we live in a world where people don't maximize their full potential?

Nicholas: It'd be easy to list a long list of negatives, but you know, we are where we are. Everyone is born into the environment in which they find themselves, and they learn through their experiences, and why is that process not faster? Well, to a degree, learning goes at it's own pace, so just as we all learn in our lives, our cultures, our institutions, and our ways of doing things learn, and what holds them back? Well, fear. Fear holds people back, although fear can be appropriate.

All of us, both as individuals and as a group, have wounds. You know, we have traumas that we've had in our lives, sometimes big traumas that are very heavy duty, and other, but certainly lots of rather smaller ones like being shamed at school or being worried what people think about you and so on. I think that all of those hold us back.

Sometimes we have limiting beliefs. For example, in economics, a lot of people are held back by thinking that there's just one pie that has to be cut up and shared out, so people spend all their time fighting over how big their slice of the cake is rather than realizing we can just make the cake a lot bigger.

Melanie: I was once at a Tony Robbins training, and this quote that he said that's always stayed with me, and I think it's really accurate in what you just said, and he had a story that there were two sons, and one was hugely successful, happy, had a fantastic life, and the other son was a complete dropout, didn't maximize his potential, wasn't working, wasn't flourishing, and he asked them both separately, "What is the reason for the way you are?"

They both gave the same answer, they said, "My father." I've always loved that story because it's empowering to know that it's yourself rather than the victim mentality, or I've had this or this happen to me or whatever, and that's why I like your project so much as well. It's about empowering people, but it is about, underneath it all, it's about self worth and the future of Western Civilization or the whole global Civilization is about self-worth, how do we get to the core of valuing ourselves and therefore our planet?

Nicholas: Wow, that's an enormous question.

Melanie: (laughs) Cup of tea?

Nicholas: How do we get ... say the question again. How do we get to ...

Melanie: I see the relationship of that story that I just told is about self worth and self value, and if we value ourselves, we value everything outside ourselves to create, we want to live in a place that is thriving and is alive, because we have that sense of ourselves. So how do we get to that point?

Nicholas: I think there's two parts. I think there's going within to directly experience one's being, so not the ego mind or the neurotic thoughts or the worries or the logical mind but directly experience the being, the one who is in, the energy that is in the body, and through that direct awareness read one's intuition that's the inner compass. Who am I? Where are we going? How do I sense things? How do I know what's right and wrong? How do I read the energy of myself and others of ideas and know what to go with? How do I make judgments? One is really up-regulating and calibrating that inner compass.

The second part is knowing the map, knowing the environment that we're in by using our full senses, using all of that intuition, all that I just described, but focused outwards in connection with others, interconnection with others, as through relating, as parents, as children, as a doctor, as a person in a shop, as a person in a company, as a member of a country, as just someone together in relation to others.

Obviously, absolutely, the logical mind of listening, thinking, knowing, learning, and being aware of our formal structures, and yes, that last bit, in connection with others, really. We are both an individual and parts of whole living system, so having our awareness turned inwards and outwards...

Melanie: Right.

Nicholas: ... and in doing that, we will naturally be drawn energetically, positively towards, I suppose, different levels of things that are a base level, desires and lusts and hungers and cravings and we use our judgment as to whether those are good for us or not and desirable. It depends on people's situation obviously, I mean, if you're seriously ill, or if you're in a famine situation, or if you're working desperately to pay the bills, you are going to have a different set of values and a different outlook to someone who's in my situation or your situation. Basically, people will find their own level appropriate to their own situation and go with what's right for them.

Also, on the negative side, you feel pain. You feel things that you don't like. Things that create fear, or things that create suffering, and then we have a desire to either avoid those or, where appropriate, to heal them or integrate them or solve them, etc. Then, at the highest level, we tap into our inspiration, our positive vision, the heaven on earth stuff, the … the unleashing of our full potential.

Melanie: I agree fully, but I think that's one side also that I know you do a lot of work, and brilliant work on the vision, there always a shadow side to people that might be pulling them down, might be self-sabotage, self-suicide, or even just a bit of distraction which can lead away from people's vision, and they might find it more exciting to live on an edge with shadow that's got all sorts of devil enticements, so to say, "Come over here, it's much more exciting."

Again, like you say, it could be through trauma or learned behavior or whatever that they've got into their shadow mission as opposed to their vision of heaven. What do you do with that?

Nicholas: Hmm. (pausing to think) There's a one-word answer. It's integration. I'm certainly very familiar with that myself, both as an individual and in those I relate to and then in our culture as a whole, and the term comes from this sort of Jungian idea that there are parts of ourselves of which we are fully aware or bits of ourselves that are driving the ship, so to speak. Then there are parts of ourselves, either which we're not aware of or which we are aware of and want to suppress or avoid or whatever. So they're pushed down out of the light into the shadow.

Essentially, the therapy answer, and I think the leadership answer is to make sure you're in a safe space and well supported, and then from that place to shine the light on those parts, and through whatever techniques you might use, for example, voice dialogue technique, but there are hundreds you could choose to bring light to those. The shadow stuff, could be alcohol, it could be gambling, it could be crime, it could be having an affair, it could be having sort of a lust for wars or hoarding money, or it could be, very commonly, an entitlement mentality or a victim mentality, and so on.

Basically, the aim is to bring the light to those, bring awareness to those, get into dialogue with those internally, or of course, on a group level, you'd be doing it at a group level, which is partly the aim of this project. There's a kind of a natural healing, really, that goes on. It's not a quick fix. I can't really summarize it quickly; it's a deep, deep work.

So for example, on a group level, in our national shadow, we've got the British mentality, we've got great patriotism and pride in our history and who we've been as a tribe, who we are as a tribe, what our role is, all the amazing things our ancestors have done and what a dynamic, vibrant place we live in, but there is a dark side to it as well. There's been, as in all humanity, there's been exploitation. There's been inequality. There's been racism. There's been social class inequality. There's been slavery, abuse of others, abuse of power, of course, as there are in all cultures.

So there's that dark side. Now, what we tend to do is polarize it, and people will either go with one or the other, so they'll either just be very patriotic, just like in an individual's self-esteem, take pride in the positive stuff and deny or push away the negative, or more commonly in our culture, people identify with the negative and list all the things that they hate about being British and all the reasons that we're bad and everything that's bad about our history and so on and kind of revel in that in almost like a self-harming or suicidal type way, and then they project the good things onto others and falsely, naively identify with the other, which is one of the pathologies of multicultural ideology.

The healthy way forward is really to get it all out on the table. Warts and all, and integrate them healthfully really. It's a process of dialogue. It's a process of healing. It's a process of judgment and of non-judgment, depending on the context, and of leadership, really, individual and collective.

Melanie: As you were speaking that, I was imagining Britain like a little person with its own little mind, and this is more about the future of

Western Civilization, so if you imagine Western Civilization being embodied in a person, and your PA says on the phone, "Excuse me, Dr.
Beecroft, we have an emergency appointment," or "Mr. or Mrs. Western
Civilization," and he or she comes shuffling in, (laughing) and he needs
emergency treatment, what would you say the state of Western Civilization as a mind, body, and soul is right now? Your big picture right here
and now?

Nicholas: Wow, that's a fantastic question. That's really good. That's
really funny. Okay, I think it must have multiple personality disorder because there are lots of different selves, all with different parts that don't
necessarily communicate and are not very integrated, I would say.
There'd be that self-loathing part that I've just referred to, you know,
the "Everything is bad, everything is falling apart."

That would be the fear-based one, so the fear state of everything is terrible, you know. The economy is in trouble, we're running out of
resources, were abusing the planet, there's so much inequality, lack of
social mobility. We've still got racism. We've got uncontrolled immigration with all the consequences of that. We've got kind of an Islamic
fundamentalist insurrection globally, which is trying to take over. We've
got lots of other countries coming up, which is great for them, but it's
kind of very risky, because they won't necessarily share our way of life
or our views, and they might take us to a rather darker place, like the
Chinese taking over, recolonizing the world as they are in Africa and
South America. The Russians are operating more at a nationalistic gang-
ster level, and so on.

Anyway, so there's that. I could go on, you know, I was getting into that
state by talking about it. There's an awful lot of people who like to think
of themselves as liberals in this culture war, the liberals and the left ver-
sus conservatives, and I see a lot on the liberal left like to think of
themselves as in the happy camp, righteous, but that's not true. They will
listen to the conservative camp, who will say, "Oh there's crime, there's
immigration problems, there's da-da-da-da-da." But they have their own
list of negatives, a very long list of negatives, and they also have a massive shadow side, including shadow racism on the left and in the liberal
mentality. So no one escapes that. We all have that part.

There's clearly the part which is still doing entrepreneurialism and capitalism absolutely dynamically, and that would have subparts. It would have the unhealthy part which would be more of the old sort of selfish, abusing, planet-destroying, human-exploiting, greedy, lying, cheating, entitled parts, which have got us into some of the troubles we've got at the moment.

But we can falsely focus on that and say, "It's all wrong, it's all bad." Well, there's a really healthy part, you know? Capitalism is an amazing, amazing force that unleashes human potential, and in places where it's well developed and well supported and well directed, it can serve any form of human potential really very, very well.

We've got the masculine parts and the feminine parts in many dimensions. Both of those have gone through huge transition. I say the feminine part ...

Melanie: That's why I'm saying it's a Mr. or Mrs. Western Civilization. I was trying to just have a little character come through door so you could just see it as a whole, because if it is a whole, we've got those little compartments, and we're always battling between male and female and that integration, so I don't want sex I'd give Western Civilization, if it's Mr. or Mrs.

Nicholas: I think a lot of people would reflexively say it's masculine. That's the New Age or the more trendy way to talk about it. I think there are two levels on which people would say that. One would be the feminist interpretation that the world used to be patriarchal, fully male-dominated. Of course, some would say it still is, and you know, the masculine has dominated the feminine, and masculine has been abusing the feminine, and now we're going through a phase of empowering the female and balancing that.

Melanie: Well, I think also the feminine has been abusing the male. I mean, there's been a whole imbalance of male and female is, I think, vital to the future of Western Civilization, and I think empowerment is just accepting who you are, whatever sex you are, and that it's good to be different, and that we work well together.

The reason I was saying Mr. or Mrs. Western Civilization was because there's always a battle between male or female, but we really need to be integrated as one and stop fighting each other, embrace our uniqueness and how we complement each other, in my opinion, work together. If a man and woman can theoretically work together, then the whole planet, male or female, it's like giving, receiving, it's a balance of combination, isn't it? It's vital for growth and for maximizing the potential, like you say.

So how do you see that?

Nicholas: Okay, so we haven't just got the man and woman on the couch, but we've got a whole room full of people, including all the children, and including elders and so on. The description that I like the most about it comes from David Deida, if you like, traditional man who, in his healthy form is strong, powerful, protective, decisive, go-getting, risk-taking, bold, sexy, embodied, warrior, and in his unhealthy form, abusive, destructive, prone to being isolated, prone to addiction, prone to being sexually abusive, disrespecting the environment, the planet, and so on.

Then, if that's traditional man, and then there's new man who's been around more prominently since the 60s, but would have gone back longer, and in his healthy form, he is sensitive and spiritual and connected and in touch with the feminine, consensus seeking and open to women, and in his unhealthy form, he is weak, indecisive, unable to defend himself, not sexy, wimpy, really. So there's the healthy positive and negative of those.

Then, there's the female equivalent of the traditional woman being, the traditional feminine being very loving, very caring, very kind, very maternal, very supportive, very interconnecting, very nurturing, and then in her unhealthy form, passive, weak, under the thumb, a bit victimy, defenseless, maybe manipulative, stuck in her little child, the equivalent of the traditional male.

Then, there's the new woman, meaning the feminist woman who came to escape those negative parts, and she would be positive strong, bold, a lot of masculine characteristics, strong just as the sensitive male had the feminine characteristics, so she's embodied strong, masculine character-istics of being determined, forceful, decisive, incisive, powerful, capable, and so on. In her unhealthy form, this the unhealthy feminism, really, so abusive, aggressive, castrating, hating men, not being nurturing, not being motherly, and really just being a man in a woman's body.

Then, so that's the majority of the population in those roles, but there are some people, and I don't pretend to be in this role myself. I think it's something which I and we aspire to do at our best is to take the healthy strands of those and integrate them into a conscious, embodied self in relation to the other gender so that the third man and third woman position of taking the positive strength of both really.

I think some people use the language of the masculine and the feminine in a kind of a mystical or spiritual sense, and they mean those kind of essences, and there's some value in that when they mean we've had the masculine period of the, you know, incisive, separated, kind of computer mentality, and so the negative masculine qualities, and we haven't had enough of the positive feminine ones. I think that's probably right.

A lot of feminism has taken on the characteristics of the old masculine, and I think what we're seeing is in both in amongst older people, amongst the most evolutionary types, the most cutting edge people, and I think also naturally, healthily emerging in the younger generations, 25 and down. They are more naturally embodying and expressing the healthy masculine and feminine at all it's levels from the child through the younger age up into the wisdom elder levels.

I think there are a lot of wounds there. There's a lot of old stuff, a lot of old battles, but I think it's really going in a healthy direction, mainly be-cause the heat's come out of the battle, and people have matured, and a lot of the wounds, if not healed, will simply die with the people who have them, and the new generations won't really be troubled by that. They'll have moved on.

Having said that, you have to put that in cultural context because, of course, a lot of people coming to Western Civilization, either physically coming or as immigrants or people where they're taking on Western

Civilization in their countries, they're not necessarily at the same stage of development in that evolution, so on a global perspective, I don't think that you could say that women are free and emancipated and so on. There's a lot of very old, dark, patriarchal stuff still going on around the world.

Melanie: If we carry on with the analogy of Mr. or Mrs. Western Civilization's come in, and you're doing your note-taking for this mind that is coming for help, what would be at the core of it? What would be the main trauma? What needs to get right in there to really help this mind and body?

Nicholas: Dehumanization.

Melanie: Can you explain that more, please?

Nicholas: Cutting off from life creates systems which treat us as if we are machines. I'll put it positively first. One of the amazing things about Western Civilization is science and reason and the way in which that has enabled us to understand the world in a way that has taken us light years ahead and created the technology that we're talking on (Skype), and we will continue to do so. It's absolutely incredible. Part of doing that means seeing the world as separate objects, each of which has properties which can be observed and tested, and then we create theories to explain the world and then test them through experiment. That's wonderful. I've got no criticism of that at all.

The flip side of that is that we've put our focus upon looking at things as external objects, and particularly we've biased ourselves towards thinking of things as physical things, and we've created a separation, Descartes' separation of mind and body as being separate, the dualism. Because of that, we tend to think that we live in a world of objects in which we're an object separate from other people who are objects. A lot of the things that we have around, like just about everything, like money or how do you train someone to be a doctor or our transport network, those things you could look at physically, but actually, 99% of it is in consciousness. It's in our mind. It's in our not just individual but collective shared mind. One of the costs of that bias is that we've cut

THE FUTURE OF WESTERN CIVILIZATION

off from our inner being and we've cut of from just the basic simplicity that we are human beings. Simple as that, we are beings and relate to each other as beings.

Melanie: Well, I enjoyed your interview with Mark Walsh about disembodiment, and I totally agree that that is a huge need for us to get back in our bodies to really, to feel where we are now and to deal with life. We've got Mr. and Mrs. Western Civilization in one body walking into your room, and so it's obviously, there's that part of them, that mind and body that you're analyzing for the future of Western Civilization, and what notes would you be taking down from looking at that part of them?

Nicholas: Which part, sorry?

Melanie: The male and female part.

Nicholas: If you look at our birth rates, and I'm included in this, if you look at the birth rates in Western countries, and also other countries that are closely aligned in terms of, I suppose, industrial culture like Japan and Russia, the birth rates—and China as well, actually—increasingly, there's sort of the middle classes in India and so on, or even Iran. Basically, when people industrialize and urbanize, there seems to be a collapse in the birth rate, partly driven by economics of maybe not needing to have so many children and also can't afford so many because in a small traditional village, the number is probably the more the merrier, but in urban and advanced industrial life, it's very costly.

But we've gone so far that we're having so few children that our population's in trouble. If you look at the white population, the original aboriginal populations of Europe, many of those are collapsing fast. For example, particularly the countries you'd least expect it, the very Catholic ones like Italy and Spain and Germany also. There are quite shocking collapses in the birth rates, and if those are not put right, then two major things will happen.

One is that a very small number of children and young people will have to shoulder the economic and the physical burden of looking after an

aging population, and that suggests our quality of life will drop significantly whilst that hump is dealt with. If it stabilizes, then in 50 years, a
lower world population might be a good thing in terms of resources
and space, but not with it happening precipitously quickly.

Also, another factor is that that process, whilst it's global, is happening to all
cultures. It's happening to cultures at different speeds, so those who first
went into the industrial revolution and the industrial age and the enlightenment and so on such as ourselves and the other Western countries
happening first, and those that it's happen last to are those that are last to
go into those phases, so that's the Middle East and Africa.

There's an issue from a security point of view because if all of those
people take on Western Civilization or broadly democracy, freedom,
education, human potential, security, respect for human rights, and so
on, then it's completely irrelevant what culture or race or religion people are. But if they don't, if they go down another path of Chinese
nationalism or Islamic fundamentalism, or if they're just simply going at a
much slower pace, then Western Civilization may drop away, may evap-
orate, may collapse before it's finally succeeded.

What's happened was with feminism and with women coming into the
workplace and coming into what used to be male roles and so on, the
difference between the genders has become much closer, so women
have become more masculinized and more taking up the male space,
and men have become more feminized, and the polarity between the
two is less because those two don't attract each other in quite the
same way as the traditional masculine and the traditional feminine.

What, I think, I'm observing in the people I meet and around me but
from a low base is that that's moving apart again, not back to the old
traditional masculine and feminine but to a more, if you like, the embodied goddess and the embodied god.

Melanie: Oh, that would be lovely.

Nicholas: In the Tantric sense, people are finding they're equal but different and obviously with full diversity in between and all the different types of

people there are, and anyone can be anything they like, but nevertheless, within that broadly speaking, men and women have distinctions and so on, and people are getting more comfortable with that really.

Anyway, soon they're going to have more babies, so you'll see that. If you look at our birth rates, the demographic graphs, you'll see that as that kicks in, Western people will have more children, and it will re-balance. In Britain, you're already beginning to see some of the signs of that, but it's from …

Melanie: I'm really excited. I'm just so really excited to read your book. I really am. It's nice to hear your voice. I know you give your views on your interviews, but it's nice to give you the same space and inquiry too, to listen to what you have to say. That's very interesting. Obviously, we can talk for hours about that, but let's move on to a bit more analysis of Western Civilization on your couch, and you're obviously taking notes and analyzing your patient, as it were. Is there anything intuitively that's disturbing you, you know, when you've got a gut feeling like thinking, "Oh, well, there's something not quite right here." What's that?

Nicholas: Well, in terms of the project, I think something that you pointed out is that my choice was to go for visionary leaders, interview visionary leaders looking to get people who've got positive, optimistic stories of who we are, where we're going, and particular domains, and to test that practically. My intention is very much to do that. There's lots more to do, but because of that, I've not been exploring the shadow side, the dark side, so much. That's partly because I wanted to focus on the positive and put the energy into the positive, but I think there is a rebalancing to be done to go more for that.

Melanie: I think that sounds juicy.

Nicholas: I think that that will involve having more juicy and more controversial people to speak to, and I think probably maybe more fiery, more sparks.

Melanie: Well, that sounds really fascinating. Can you tell me a bit more, how you'd like to go about doing that?

Nicholas: Not, really, no. You can ...

Melanie: Watch this space.

Nicholas: You can watch and see.

Melanie: Oh, good. Why do you always call it the future of Western Civilization? Why not future of the planet earth or Civilization?

Nicholas: That's a great question. A lot of people have said that to me by way of feedback, and the reason for that is that the starting point I had was, I suppose I grew up to be patriotically British, and we do operate on a nation state level traditionally, and so the obvious place for my political mind was British and British politics, and so on, but I found that when I began to look at our culture and what the things that are going on, I had this naïve idea that I could look to other countries to find alternative models and systems, variety and experimentation.

For example, when I was looking at the machine model of management, the way that our hospitals are run as if they were made up of cogs and spreadsheets and numbers as opposed to human beings, both as patients and as staff. I naively imagined that all I could look around to Sweden or look to New Zealand or wherever, and there would be really dynamic people doing something very different.

What shocked me was, whether in that area or discipline in schools, or taxation, or anything, bizarrely, we're missing a trick. We're part of a much larger culture, a group consciousness and most of them are doing the same things too. To look at it just on a British level, it doesn't make sense because we are part of a much bigger group, and of course, you could look at it as London or doctors or male doctors or London or, you know, my family, or the immediate community. All of these, you know, I think the truth is, it's nested. We live on many levels.

I think it became clear to me that we were operating on, at the very least, the English-speaking world, mainly Britain, America, Canada, Australia, New Zealand, South Africa, and those people who speak English in all the other countries, really including India, Sri Lanka, Singapore,

179

Hong Kong, much of Africa and so on. Really, it's more than that. I think the same phenomena, a lot of the same phenomena are happening throughout the Europe and really throughout the rest of the world. So why not then make it global?

To a degree we are globalizing and we are, we do live in a global world, and we are integrating, and we're interconnecting but we're not there yet, and I think that will probably, unless we rally mess up badly, economically or militarily or whatever, it is going to a global world, and that's a good thing, and eventually the world will be one living system made up of interconnected living beings, and all the different parts of it, whether that the be London or Britain or whatever, will be just like a node in the consciousness, just like a group of birds in the bigger flock.

I think as we are now, there are still things which are very distinct, and for me, thinking about it just on a British level is too small. Some things need to be thought of on a global level.

For example, if you talk about political correctness or multicultural ideology, that doesn't mean anything in Argentina, does it? I don't know. I don't know. Maybe it does. I don't really think so. I don't think they're really at the stage of doing stuff like that. If you're looking at what are we going to do with our economy, well, in Brazil, they've got different issues. So there are things particular to the West. We're all mixing up and interconnecting, and through immigration, but we're all still a very distinct societies. Some people have said it's big-headed to have a project called The Future of Western Civilization, because it sounds so megalomaniac, but I think it would be arrogant to assume I could speak for all the rest.

I don't know a lot about Africa, China or the non-Western world. I mean, I know some things. I've got a healthy interest in them, and I've been there, but you know, we are still different, and we all do still have a distinct consciousness and distinct values and so on.

British is too small. These processes are happening on a much bigger scale. Many processes are happening on a global scale, but on balance, I think that the West is distinct enough to talk about on that level.

I think if I just said global Civilization, a lot of the things which I think we need to sort out wouldn't be of interest elsewhere. How are we going to sort out our healthcare system? In Malawi, they would like a health care system. It's a different scenario. We are all humans, but we do live in different places and have particular situations and life conditions, so it's not that I don't care about those people or don't think we're going global.

I'll put it another way. I'd say that's stretching it quite far. Most traditional things have only focused on the national level or on a class-based level or a gender-based level, and so to stretch is a big as Western Civilization is pretty huge.

Melanie: Thank you for clarifying that. You often talk about fractals and say we're in this living system, but surely, we already are in a living system, and sometimes when you talk about it, you say ... it's like "when we get to that point," so what's going wrong that the fractal level if isn't working now, that were not yet complete? I know what you're trying to say is that when it's really striving and working and connecting that we will just flourish and the potential is huge, but as it stands right now, it is working on some level, whether it be dysfunctional or not, so why is that?

Nicholas: Well, I think you're absolutely right, that yes, we are already in a living system. I'm alive, and you're alive, and so is everyone else. That's right. That's right. So it already exists, but the shift is of being aware of it, being conscious of it, and acting as if it were true. That's the shift. So it's already true. It's being aware of it.

To make that practical, for example, at the moment, I'm doing a project with an organization looking at their outcome measures, which might sound a bit dull, but traditionally, they've looked at their outcome measures as if it were a machine. It's a very human system providing a human medical service, so it's got medical staff and patients and a wider network, and the traditional way of looking at it is to treat it as if it's a machine, an object like boxes with lines drawn between them, and sets of processes, and to measure medical productivity according to bums on seats. How many people do you see? How fast do you see them?

That's all fine. I wouldn't take away from that, but the problem with seeing it in a way that can be reduced to a spreadsheet is that we're missing out on what's already there, and already, that team is operating with its patients and with all the other people that it serves, and there are already outcome measures embedded in the system, imbedded in every relationship.

So every time someone sees a patient, or every time someone from a different organization interacts with them, and they provide a service to them, even if no one says it, even if no one writes it down, even if no one puts a number on it, there is an authentic outcome measure integrated into that. At it's most crude level, if that team did something really wrong, someone would phone up the boss and do something about it. Or it would hit the media, or someone in the hierarchy would say, "Oi, what's going on here?" A patient might report somebody.

So those are kind of negative examples, but people get praise. People get praised for things, and anyway, the point is that there is a living system there, so the people are constantly, through their interactions, relating to one another. But if you have a mindset where you think of it as a machine, so here we have a structure made up of cogs, and what's their output, and how do we measure them as statistics, and how do we put them in a spreadsheet, that's okay, but no only that.

But if you only do that, then you miss on the huge depth and richness that there is by realizing that you've got an amazing living system made up of conscious beings constantly interacting with one another. It's kind of a limiting belief, so I agree with you. It's not about moving to a living system. It's about getting rid of our limiting beliefs or our lack of low expectations and realizing that we're in a living system.

Melanie: What are the limiting beliefs, do you think, the Western mind has about itself?

Nicholas: The first one that came to me was that growth has to be about money. That's very obvious. The way we've designed our financial system, our economic system, assumes that we have to have constant growth, more and more money and more and more consumption, and the problem with that is obvious that, you know, there's limited resources. Of course, we will improve technology, but there eventually is a finite limit.

When people are poor, they definitely need more to be happy or to be secure, no question about that, but beyond a certain level, actually that's not the most important thing. Our belief that we need money to be happy or that we need ever-increasing material possessions is a limiting belief, because that isn't necessarily for security or human potential or fun or love or sex or community and so on.

Melanie: As the Mr. or Mrs. Civilization's on your couch, you're diagnosing in your head and writing notes, are you giving it labels, or diagnoses from your psychiatrist point of view?

Nicholas: No, I think that would be over the top, stretching the metaphor too far. Not really.

Melanie: Well, I know you're not a labels kind of person anyway. What's the treatment program? What the journey of recovery if it needs recovery?

Nicholas: Great question. What is the treatment program?

We could dive into lots of specifics, but the biggest picture, it's awareness, integration, and healing, so bringing awareness to all the different parts—the healthy, the unhealthy, the known, the unknown, the positive, the negative—drawing together all the different strands. Healing: What needs to be healed, and going with what needs to be done, really getting the blocks out of the way about human potential and really tapping into our pure energy and potential really. That sounds a bit simplistic, but at the biggest picture, that's it.

Same as for an individual.

Melanie: So really, that's really hopeful and, I think, a picture that we're capable of. I mean—

Nicholas: And we are doing.

Melanie: What are the parts that Western Civilization could relapse on or get stuck into, from your point of view?

Nicholas: Well, the economic situation is very precarious, partly because of the unsustainable debt situation, and partly just because for historical reasons, because the way we've developed, we're very imbalanced economically with the rest of the world, and there's going to have to be a reckoning, a rebalancing, no question about that. That could happen in a precipitous cataclysmic way in which all of our structures fall apart. We could end up with whole government systems really failing, and real poverty, and real sickness.

Of course, we don't exist in a vacuum. Other players may interact, such as the stuff that's happening in the Middle East may well spill over into Europe. We could have a lot of descent into crime and so on. So if that happens, then our mindset will inevitably and necessarily shift down into security and survival, and in that, challenges of that order might be wonderful for stimulating really amazing leaps into new ways of doing things, but equally, they can take you to very dark places with a lot of killing and a lot of hate and a lot of collapse. So there are really scary outcomes, which are possible.

Melanie: I do find it interesting that if you look at the image of the Western Civilization as the mind and the body and the soul, and then an embodiment, as it were, and then looking at it, in the past, we've had wars between countries, between members of families, to nations, to countries, but now, the war is on terror, and I'm sure most of us all experience some kind of fear or panic personally in our own bodies, but to have a whole Western Civilization where the war is on terror, it's not really specific, is it? How do we cope with that? How do we cope with the Western mind full of terror?

Nicholas: Yes, I thought about that the other day because yesterday I was out in Central London with a friend, and we were in by the Dome, the Millennium Dome, and there was a small bang. I don't even know what it was, but everyone jumped and looked, and it made me realize that even though it was a beautiful sunny day, unlike it has been for the rest of the year, people were having a great time, and there were tourists from all over the world and all over the country there, a really lovely atmosphere.

Just under the surface, there is that fear, and people would, you know, go "What's that? What have they done now?" etc. That's real. That dark stuff is there. What do we do about it?

Well, several levels, really. Well, many levels, many layers. I spent years obsessing about the War on Terror, stimulated by September the 11th, realizing, "What the hell are we going to do about this? This is really scary." For a long while, my focus was on what I called "Psyplomacy," which is the psychological dimension of our foreign policy, which is actually an example of becoming aware of the living system of which we're a part. It's understanding foreign policy and international relations as a living system.

The traditional way of looking at it was the relationship between one King and another or one diplomat and another, and so on, and more recently it's the relationship between institutions, like between one Foreign Office and another, or a bunch of diplomats in the UN, etc.

All that's true, but the way that they've operated traditionally was to have two main dimensions. One was force, the ability to physically force the other to do what you want; military power, and the second part was transactional; doing deals, doing trade, legal agreements, contracts; it could be a Machiavellian level of operation, or it could be a legal contract level of operation.

Now, a lot of people would say, "Oh, that's all bad." It's not bad. It's absolutely fine. Those are real dimensions of the world, but the one that September the 11th made realize was that we were not giving enough attention to is what's the third dimension.

All human relationships have at least three dimensions: the potential for force, transactional, but of course then, there's the, if you like, the love level. The being-to-being level. The interconnection level, and also the hate level. The emotional level. That's the level at which we trust people, we decide whether we trust them or not, whether we like them or not, whether we identify with them or not, whether we want to be with them, whether we feel secure around them, and of course, that happens between individuals, but ever increasingly, it happens at a mass consciousness level.

185

It always did. You could go back to 15th Century England and say, "What do you think of the Africans?" I think they called them Moors, and people would have some idea, but of course, based virtually totally on prejudice and myth, and very few would ever have met someone from there. Whereas now, the degree to which we're interconnected, both physically meeting each other, traveling to each other's countries, migrating, and so on, and the media, crucially, and the internet, we really have got mass interconnection.

Anyway, the point was, I spent years looking at this. I thought the solution was simply, that we need to have better understanding with the Islamic world, so between the West and the Islamic world, we need better understanding. We need mutual respect. Building trust, building confidence in one another, and so on. If we do that, then it'll all be a happy outcome.

I still agree with that. That's all still true, but there's a big "*but*," and there's a big "*and*." There's a "*but*" that's not enough, "*and*" there's a lot more that we need. What I concluded was that our focus in the War on Terror was to, first off, mainly be in a fear state and to focus our fear upon the other, in other words the Muslims or the Islamic world, and work out what we need to do to manipulate them to get them to do what we want. The mechanisms we used were either military, the first dimension or manipulation, the second-to think through marketing ways of thinking, how do we package and market what we want them to do and get them to do it, or how do we manipulate the system and so on.

There's some validity in those mechanisms, but the way the world is now, that's not enough, and that's not really going to work. What I noticed was that there was a massive great big hole in that you can't really do dialogue and relations with someone else if you don't know who you are yourself. So if the Western world is trying to relate to the Islamic world, and we do that from kind of two positions, those two I mentioned earlier.

One is like the last remnants of the old way, which is the "We're superior, we're right, we know best," you know, a distorted view of science and capitalism and progress, and you know, "They're primitives, and we will manipulate them to get what we want and use power to achieve it, whether economic or physical." They're not going to like that. That doesn't mean it's wrong, but there's going to be a backlash from that, and the world is evening out, and they're getting a lot more powerful, so they're going to be doing that back, both directly and asymmetrically. We need to operate in that space, but that's not going to be enough.

Then there's the other dimension, which is a bit like the male and female, like the sensitive man or the position, which is the politically correct, multicultural self, which is to say we don't even exist. If you say, "Who's we? How can you say we? What do you mean British? Oh no, you can't say that? We're just global." It's the self-hating. "We hate ourselves. Everything we've ever done is wrong. All men are wrong. All doctors are wrong. All authority is wrong. Christianity is bad. Capitalism is abusive. There is no truth. You must not judge anything unless you disagree with me, in which of course you're in serious trouble."

Then, in comes immigration into that space, and then those people who've come to the West for a better life, whether it be economic or better human rights, opportunity, values, culture, or because they're running away from something that they don't like, if they then arrive into that space, and they're told by one group, "You're a bunch of foreigners and primitives," the old racist mindset. "You can never be a member of our group, but we'll patronize you and pat you on the head and throw you a few crumbs off the table as long as you're good."

Then the other group, the second group, are the ones who say, "Oh, we completely hate ourselves. There is no such thing as Britain or Britishness. We're just a multicultural melting plot in which every culture is celebrated, apart from our own. We hate ourselves. We don't exist." Then all these people are treated in a shadow racist way. They're invited in and put on a false pedestal. "Oh, your nonwhite so you're good, you're special, you're nice." You know? "You're culture, we used to oppress it, so we now celebrate it as a font of all wisdom and goodness." That's racist, actually, and it's really stupid and naïve and childish.

But that's what multiculturalism does, and it encourages those people to perceive themselves as victim groups who are then given a special status in relation to the oppressor group, and lots of laws are created so that the oppressor group can't make any criticism or judgment of the victim group, and the victim group are given special laws to give them preferential treatment and so on, and if you're in that group, not surprisingly, you'd have no respect for the people you've just come amongst.

One bunch are the racist and dominating control freaks who think you're nothing and won't ever let you join them, and the other group, these days rather larger, are the group of people who've got no self esteem, who hate themselves and think we're nothing, and probably, you're quite poor or on the poorer end of society, so you also meet those bits of society which are really messed up, into drink, drugs and dysfunctional behavior.

Imagine yourself as a taxi driver in a northern city in Britain picking people up on a Friday night, and all you can see is a load of girls dressed like prostitutes, and all the guys drunk, vomiting up their kebabs in the back of the taxi, and then going home to your family, who come from a traditional foreign background, who still got some culture, who've still got authority and respect and so on. It's not surprising they would reject the space they've come into.

So that's a lot of background. My conclusion? What's the therapy? The therapy is that we need to sort ourselves out. We need to finish off these last remnants of the old domination of the racist mindset. We are human beings. We are all one. We are all interconnected. Race is completely irrelevant. It isn't yet irrelevant practically because of history and geography and so on, but at the highest level, it's irrelevant, and we need to get rid of all of that shadow nonsense, all of that inversion of the old mindset, which is just turn the old stuff on it's head.

We need to work out, who are we? Both me, you, us as a group, as a nation, as a Civilization, as a globe? Where are we going? What is right? What is wrong? What is true? What is false? We need to make judgments on a daily basis. Judgments are good. They're not just bad. We can't live in a world of non-judgment. You need judgment just to know whether to eat a bit of chicken that smells a bit funny. You need judgment to work out whether you're going to cross the road when someone looking who's frightening you is coming to you? Is it safe? You need to judge, make a judgment about what I think of the suicide risk of this patient, or can I trust this banker with my investment? So at the core of it, we in the West need to rejuvenate our identity, our culture, our authority, our wisdom, our sense of right and wrong, our sense of morality, our entrepreneurialism, our balance between the masculine and the feminine, the way that we are living beings, the way that we've responded to life.

We need to sort out and rebalance our economy. We need to sort out and rebalance our education system, and so the core of it, basically if we are really successful and dynamic and attractive, those people are not going to want to fight us. They will continue to want to come here to join us and be a part of us. If we can have a society which is both patriotic and self-confident and open to others at the same time, which requires security, both inner and group security, then were onto a winner.

If we close off and get into a them and us mindset, a polarizing mindset, and if we're arrogant, or if we're self-loathing, then we're finished.

Melanie: That was fantastic. That kind of summarized everything for the whole of Western Civilization then, not just the War on Terror, but it's a really good place to end our interview, I think. That really expresses everything that you're trying to do, where you're going, what you're doing with your project and informing and helping everyone.

How can people find the other interviews and find your other books?

Nicholas: Thank you, yes. Yes, the easiest way is to go to my website, www.nicholasbeecroft.com. It's all on the website. There's a Facebook group, a LinkedIn group and you can follow on Twitter.

I'd like to acknowledge the huge amount of help and support I've had from a lot of people, not least yourself providing lots of advice, encouragement, and guidance and support behind the scenes, and too many individuals to name, really. Many, many people have been very generous in contacting me on Facebook, Twitter, and just direct by email, offering encouragement and suggestions for interviews, putting themselves forward, and a lot of really good mentoring in the background, for example, from Don Beck, Martin Rutte, Matthew McGuinness and Howard Donenfeld in particular, so thanks to all of them. (see Acknowledgements)

Melanie: Well, thank you for letting me put you in the hot spot, and hopefully, we'll catch up again in the near future and see where you've taken it even further. It is very exciting, and I just wish you, from all your readers, just wish you all the best. We're behind you and excited with what you're coming up with, definitely excited about the book, Analyze West so let us know when that's going to come out, and well done, congratulations. It's something you should be really proud of. It's amazing.

Nicholas: Thank you.

Melanie: Thank you.

Other Books in the Series

The Future of Western Civilization series is available in four books in paperback and ebook. Each interview is also available as a separate ebook. You will find them on the main online book retailers.

www.FutureofWesternCivilization.com

Future of Western Civilization Series 1, Book 1

Introduction to the Series

British Patriotism
A Newcomer's Perspective

The Next Big Shift
From Machine to Living System

Global Simultaneous Policy Making
Bottom-Up Global Policy

The Future of Capitalism
Getting What We Really Want

Transpartisan Politics
The Power of Integrating Diversity

Creating Heaven on Earth
Taking Small Steps in the Right Direction

Bonds, Fields and Intentions
Culture Catches Up with Science

Leadership with Integrity
How to be True to Yourself

Wisdom
Lost and Rediscovered

The Living Universe
Bringing Science, Finance and Society to Life

Organizational Democracy
10 Steps to Democratic Culture and Leadership

Future of Western Civilization Series 1, Book 2

The West is Best
Insights from the PR Man to the Stars

Evolutionary Enlightenment
Living from your Creative Impulse

Renaissance 2
Catalyzing the Second Renaissance.

Positive Patriotism
The Evolving British

The Master Code
The Theory that Explains Everything

Future of Western Civilization Series 1, Book 3

Generational Cycles
Predicting the Future

Catalyzing Change
Engaging Emergence

Successful Nations
Harnessing the Aspirations of the People

Resurrecting Christianity
Rising to the Challenges of a Complex World

German Identity & Patriotism
Healing the Wounds, Integrating the Shadow.

Compassionate Healthcare
Re-humanising Medicine

New Money
The Evolution of Finance

Contact & Social Media

Thank you so much for reading the Future of Western Civilization. Please do get in touch to share your comments. Please visit the websites below.

www.FutureofWesternCivilization.com

www.nicholasbeecroft.com

http://www.facebook.com/groups/438696922812104/

http://twitter.com/Future_of_West

http://www.linkedin.com/groups?gid=4400956

Write a review

If you really enjoyed the book and the series, then please do tell your friends, share on social media and do please post reviews on Amazon, Goodreads, Kobo, Barnes & Noble, Sony, Smashwords etc. It'll help others decide whether to get a copy for themselves. If you have found any typos, awful grammar or anything else I can put right, please email me directly and I'll do so.

Best wishes,
Nicholas

www.ingramcontent.com/pod-product-compliance
Lightning Source LLC
Chambersburg PA
CBHW060503290526
45791CB00001B/249